MAFIA
MINISTRY
A CRYING SHAME

**MANIPULATION
ABUSE
FINANCES
INTIMIDATION
ARROGANCE**

CHERYL BROWN

iUniverse, Inc.
Bloomington

MAFIA MINISTRY
A CRYING SHAME

iUniverse books may be ordered through booksellers or by contacting:

iUniverse
1663 Liberty Drive
Bloomington, IN 47403
www.iuniverse.com
1-800-Authors (1-800-288-4677)

ISBN: 978-1-4620-0915-2 (pbk)
ISBN: 978-1-4620-0916-9 (ebk)

Printed in the United States of America

iUniverse rev. date: 05/06/2011

Dedication

IN MEMORY OF

MY LOVING FATHER ROY

MY BEAUTIFUL NIECE
DARNEASHA

MY "TO THE POINT
UNCLE" SINGLETON

INTRODUCTION

Hi, my name is Cheryl Brown, and the reason I wrote *MAFIA MINISTRY, A Crying Shame* is to shed light on spiritual abuse by "pastors" and televangelists who preach one thing on TV yet live another type of lifestyle off the screen and pulpit. *MAFIA MINISTRY, A Crying Shame* is a memoir based on the true accounts of when I first came into the world of "Christian ministry". I found hope in the prosperity teachings and started to wholeheartedly give my all to the "ministry": my heart, money, time, mind, body and soul. The prosperity gospel was being taught to me heavily and I was in it knee deep, devoted to such concepts as "naming it and claiming it ," "sowing seeds of money," and "sacrificially giving," all while the pastors are styling and profiling. You can't even pay your bills because you constantly are pushed to give money. You better not dare ask them for help with anything. I was leaving a domestic violence relationship when I came into the church, and other abuses had taken place in my life from as far back as I can remember. I was a very vulnerable and broken person.

I went on to work for one of the most famous televangelists in the world today, Pastor Benny Hinn. I worked as a maid for him and his family in his parsonage and television studio. I also was a member of his "church" at World Healing Center Church at the hands of his unqualified son-in-law Michael Koulianos, and his daughter Jessica. My son and I endured several levels of emotional and spiritual abuses from Benny Hinn Ministries. That eventually led me into the wrong hands of other "ministries" which ultimately abused me further. It has been five years since I left Pastor Benny's home, and I have just gotten to the point where I have been able to not constantly live in fear of them hurting me anymore.

I spent all of these years suffering mentally, physically, emotionally, financially, socially, but most of all spiritually because of all of the abuse I endured stemming from the hands of Benny Hinn and his "ministry". He is a charismatic master of deception and manipulation and he is ruthless! He has caused many sheep to suffer as he arrogantly lives in lavishness and steps on the necks of the feeble and poor. He loves to be served. There are many Benny Hinn followers all over the world that send money into his ministry and several other ministries like his. I can give you a firsthand account that your money cannot be trusted with Benny Hinn.

He "curses" anyone that goes "against" his "ministry" but today I have the boldness to come out and let the chips fall where they may. This has been a journey of recovery for me and my son. I would like anyone that find themselves or knows someone that is dealing with spiritual abuse to get help immediately. Spiritual abuse is on the rise today in every part of the world. **These predators must be stopped!** This book should be for 18 years and up unless under the direction of an adult.

Benny Hinn

Contents

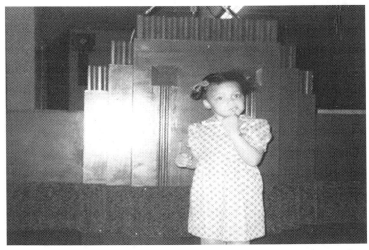

I believe that I hadn't been violated as of yet on this picture , if not it would be my last memory of how I viewed the world as a child, looks as though even then, I was trying to figure out this church business.

1

INITIATION INTO THE MINISTRY

I will never forget the brutality of the beating I endured that night: the punches, the stomping as I was knocked to the ground, the pungent odor of grass and dirt being forced up my nostrils as I was dragged by my hair. I had just been beaten pretty badly due to an altercation with my ex-boyfriend. It was at that moment when I was first initiated into the world of Christian ministry. I had come from a life of total dysfunction that included sexual, physical, and emotional abuses from as far back as I could remember. The abuse came from my mother, family, friends, boyfriends, teachers and a doctor.

It was spring of 2004 and after this particular episode, I was driving down the street at approximately two in the morning along the southeast side of Chicago near Lake Michigan. Devastated, my life was flashing before my eyes, and I had my young son in the back seat of the vehicle. Sobbing uncontrollably, I was contemplating suicide by driving into Lake Michigan.

A woman was driving in the opposite direction as me. As she was approaching me I just happened to notice her saying to me, "Do you want to pray?" I read her lips and everything seemed like a blur. I nodded my head "yes," and pulled my car over to the side of the street. We got out of our cars and stood on the sidewalk and she immediately began to pray for me. When she placed her hand on my head I lifted my arms upward, crying out to God in desperation. Having been beaten outside and dragged on the ground, I had dirt all over my checkered black-and-white chef pants and white chef jacket I had worn to culinary school that day. My hair was all over my head and I had bruises all over my face and body. I didn't care about that at that point; all that mattered to me was that God had sent someone to let me know that He cared for me. God wanted me to *live*. I began to feel a connection with God like never before and for the first time in my life I felt true love.

The woman (I will call her Tee) invited me to attend a play called Jesus of Nazareth at her church in Munster, Indiana, called Family Christian Center (FCC) with Pastor Steve Munsey. I was concerned about my appearance but assured by Tee that it didn't matter. My son and I went, yet I was still feeling embarrassed. I wore sunglasses because my eyes were black.

The church was spectacular! It was unlike any other church I had been in. The people that stood at the front door to greet you were extremely friendly. They smiled and looked as if they did not have a worry in the world. I couldn't believe it was even a church … it looked like a theater, with concession stands and Starbucks coffee … wow! It was awe-inspiring. There were a lot of people there.

As I entered the sanctuary, a different feeling came over me. Tee told me that it was the power of GOD. Nervously I held my son's hand as we found our seats up in the balcony. The lights were dimmed and the play began.

They had horses and camels on the set! It was my first time seeing anything like this and I was blown away! The play described everything that Jesus went through before and after he was hanged and crucified on the cross; how he suffered. It touched me deeply because I had never experienced the story told quite like that before. I was moved. Taking note of my reaction, Tee invited me to the church the following day, which was a Sunday.

My son and I went to church. I was able to put him into their children's ministry. The choir was awesome! I listened intently to the sermon. I did not completely understand the message because I was overwhelmed by this "different concept" of the church, and I was still numb from my beating. When the service ended, I felt an emotional awakening in my bosom. I went to the altar for prayer.

There were security guards surrounding the pastor. I stood in line to see him, and when it was my turn, I told the pastor that I was getting out of a domestic violence situation. I let him know that I was serious about rededicating my life to the Lord. I was in total surrender as he laid his hands on my head and prayed with me. My heart skipped a beat as he told me that a miracle was going to happen in three days. I was so thrilled. I was very encouraged, and as we left the church I walked and talked with Tee about how I had to get away from Chicago and out of the apartment that I was in.

On the way home from church, Tee and I saw a charming little two-bedroom, one-bath white house for rent. It was only a few minutes away from the church in Lansing, Illinois, which was right next to the Indiana border. We got out of the car when we saw the house, went and laid our hands on it, and claimed it in prayer. I had never known about the concept of "naming it and claiming it" until I went to FCC. The concept was based on word of faith and prosperity gospel teachings.

According to Pastor Munsey, "naming it and claiming it" was the practice of speaking positive things over our lives and planting seeds for them to come forth. We then claimed them as if they were already ours. For example, he taught us that if we planted seeds of money in faith that God will bless us with riches. The more money that we could sacrifice, the greater the blessing would be!

The amount of seed money revealed our level of faith. For those of us that did not sow seeds of money, there would only be poverty and mishaps. In other words, the most likely reason many of us were poor, on welfare, couldn't pay our bills, or were having all sorts of problems with our health and families was because we did not sow seeds.

So, when I first laid hands on the house, this was something new to me! I was a little intimidated at first because I was jobless at the time and had Section 8 housing, which was a subsidized housing program by the government that allowed me to move anywhere in the United States that accepted the program, and help make my rent affordable.

I had never lived in a house before; I had lived in apartments my entire life. In addition, my kindergarten-aged son and I received food stamps and welfare payments to help make ends meet. I called the landlord in faith, met with him, filled out the paperwork and waited to see what would happen.

Sure enough, the owner of the home accepted my situation and a few days later, I signed a lease agreement. My son and I were able to move into our first house. Not only were we thrilled to live there, it gave me peace of mind to know that I was right down the way from my new church home.

FCC was a nondenominational church and Pastor Steve Munsey taught the prosperity gospel to the max. Pastor Munsey was a very encouraging pastor that gave me a lot of hope. He was also very entertaining; his sermons were very dramatic. And there was always some sort of event taking place at the church like plays, parades, concerts etc. There was never a dull moment at FCC.

I was so excited about having a fresh start. While looking for work and attending culinary school, I decided to put my skills to work at the church. Since I loved to cook and bake, I began volunteering for various services at the church, including departments concerning food. I baked muffins and cookies in the morning for Starbucks and cashiered at Starbucks. I also prepared foods and worked in the concession stands during special events like plays.

The plays were a special treat to me because my son began to get involved in the church's theater program. He even got to be in the Jesus of Nazareth play there the next year! I was so honored that my son was able to be involved in theater and discover another of his natural talents and passions.

My son after the Jesus of Nazareth play at FCC

My son on the set of the Jesus of Nazareth play at FCC

One thing my pastor emphasized in his teachings was that we should serve in the house of God. The one event that stood out from all of the rest was helping to feed the homeless in Chicago. I had zeal to serve like never before. I was grateful to have the opportunity to help minister to the people, because I knew what it was like to be homeless as a child and an adult. I was a teen alcoholic and a survivor of many abusive situations, so I felt I could connect with those who were facing difficulty in life.

Various ministers had gathered together to pray with people and give them boxed lunches on the west side of Chicago. My church, FCC, was one of them along with Benny Hinn Ministries and the Monument of Faith with Pastor Richard Henton. These ministries all supported each other; and there was a very strong connection between them.

Several people were walking down the streets and sitting on the corners. I was also strolling up and down the street with my son, witnessing to them about the love of Jesus, and then I would direct them across the street to the food and ministers. I was finding my niche while teaching my son about being grateful, living a clean life, and loving people.

After this event, I was preparing to return home when a man approached me. I was walking back to the car in the parking lot with my son and Tee. The man smiled as he told me that he was one of Pastor Benny's security guards, and that their ministry had been impressed with my outreach service as a volunteer. I took it as a compliment and was encouraged by his kindness.

He began to explain further and prophesied to me, telling me that the Lord was going to do a mighty work in my life! He told me how he had seen the fire of the Lord upon me and the Lord's anointing!

By that time, I was in tears and praising the Lord for the message. Then the security guy, Benny Hinn's daughter Jessica Hinn, and her fiancé Michael Koulianos walked towards my son and me and circled around us. They laid hands on us, and they each prayed and prophesied exclusively for my son and me. I always felt that my son was going to be a great man of God, and having them saying the same thing to me was confirmation.

They told me that I was going to minister to the nations and do mighty things for the kingdom of God! I was starting to feel like the favor of the Lord was on me just as Pastor Munsey taught me. I felt very special and called for the Lord's work.

Jessica and Michael told me that if I ever needed anything to just let them know. Jessica even gave me 300 dollars cash. Wow! I was very grateful and thanked the Lord for His favor on my life. I thought *Lord, why me*? I felt that after all the pain and suffering I had endured in my life that some of the burdens were finally beginning to lift off of me. I felt a peace that I never knew. To top it off, I was so excited that she gave me money. I had literally only had three dollars in my pocket that day and I had just spent it on bottles of water for my son and a couple of other ladies from FCC, so to get 300 dollars, I thought, *now that is multiplication*! Just like Pastor Munsey taught about. I was numb and weeping tears of joy the entire ride back home.

Tee was so excited for me. She and I had such great faith. As our faith increased, we frequently went into car dealerships and upscale neighborhoods that we wanted to live in in order to "name and claim" our stuff. We would pray and cry and thank God for them in advance, and we did not let our current circumstances affect what we knew was ours!

According to the prosperity gospel, we were supposed to speak those things into existence as though they were already ours! So with all of our hearts, we believed and named and claimed what we wanted. Tee and I prayed over the 300 dollars I got from Jessica, and I decided to give 50 to FCC as a special offering. I believed that this money had multiplication all over it. I even wrote on the offering envelope "from the holy hands of Jessica Hinn."

I then put 150 dollars of it into a plastic bag, as Tee and I concluded that the Lord wanted me to bury it underneath the house I was claiming. The home was a new construction: a big, beautiful home right down the street from the church in Munster, Indiana. She even put a marking on the area so that I would know where we planted it.

For months, I would go and pray on this house every time I got out of church. Sometimes I would even go inside and pray. And no matter how broke I got, I resisted the temptation to dig up the money so the Lord wouldn't think I had little faith. One time Tee got a bottle of water to sprinkle throughout the inside and outside of the home. We walked around the house several times and prayed. She was in the choir and seemed to be a very prophetic woman of God. She had prayed on the rental house with me, was praying on the new house with me, and when I was called out and prophesied over from the event in Chicago with Jessica and Michael, she was with me. So I was really starting to believe in the prophetic realm! Things were happening and I was ready for miracles galore!

Meanwhile, Jessica and her fiancé invited me to visit a local church the next day down in Chicago called the Monument of

Faith where Richard Henton was the pastor. I had grown up watching this pastor on TV with my dad, which was one of my pleasant childhood memories. I had never visited his church before. Boy, the place was packed, it seems the people had thought that Pastor Benny himself would be speaking there that evening, but it was just Jessica and her fiancé speaking.

Jessica and I got to speak after service, and I got to tell her that I had buried the money as a seed for the home that I was claiming. I also showed her a piece of rock from the house. She called it crazy faith! She smiled and told me that she admired my strong faith level. She told me that the house was already mine, and that she couldn't wait to visit it once I moved in and have dinner with me! That was encouraging to hear from someone who was as prosperous as her father and family was. My faith was supercharged! We talked a bit, then Jessica invited me to come to the Miracle Crusade that her father was having in Chicago at the United Center. I was so happy to get the invitation. She even got me VIP seating for each service that was happening that weekend. I was stunned. I had never been to a miracle crusade before!

On the way into the service inside the United Center, I felt like an ant trying to go up against lions. People were everywhere, with their Bibles and crosses around their necks, pushing people in wheelchairs while security tried to handle the flow of people coming through the doors. I found out once I was inside the building that some people had been waiting for hours for the doors to open!

Getting through security was a nightmare, and it was extremely difficult to get to the VIP section. When I told security that Jessica had me on the VIP list, they said "Yeah right; do you think we believe you?" It was as though I were at a Michael Jackson concert. I told them I was telling the truth, and sure enough, the security verified my name on the VIP list and let me through. I got to my seat and all the seemingly important people in the ministry were there: pastors from around the city along with their wives and staff. I felt sort of out of place at first because some people were speaking in tongues, while others were on their knees wailing. They seemed super deep!

The choir was looking beautiful on the stage. It was a mass choir composed of singers from around the city, and it was huge. The singing started and the atmosphere became electrified. Everyone was singing praises to the Lord, and then I began to feel more comfortable. I love to sing praises to the Lord.

I was worshipping the Lord, and my eyes were closed with my arms lifted. I was really into it. I believe we were singing "How Great Thou Art." Then the people started getting excited because Pastor Benny Hinn had finally walked on the stage in a white suit. *Wow!* I thought. *The man himself.*

Now I was in the VIP section in the middle, close to the front, on the floor level and all of the people in wheelchairs were to the right of me all bunched together. I wondered why they had to sit in one section all together; I thought to myself that they should be in the VIP section, not me. But, just like everyone else, it seemed that they were just happy to be in the building.

The service was nothing like I had ever experienced. My faith level was high and there was something about all of those people coming together to pray with expectation in their hearts that got to my very core.

Pastor Benny spoke with authority in his voice. He cast out demonic forces, he gave us hope, he took an offering and then he began to go into the realm where people would believe for their healing. The atmosphere was mystical.

When it came time to tell how we were healed, I even got in the line. My ear had popped during the service and something felt like it literally lifted off of me. I had been having migraine headaches for a while so I thought it was amazing that I felt this different lightness, sort of like weights being lifted off of me!

As you stand in line, workers come up and ask you what your miracle was; I assumed that they chose who they want to come up on the stage with Pastor Benny. I couldn't believe my eyes. There were so many people fighting to get up to the front where he was. Pastor Benny would wave his hand like a wand and people would fall out as if they had been "slain in the spirit." And when everyone fell down in the crowd from the waving of his hand, I fell too. I did not know if it was from the anointing or just getting knocked down, but I got up with a huge bruise on my bottom that lasted for weeks.

I was amazed and wanted to know what it all meant. I was feeling the spirit. I even brought a picture of my brother who was disabled from a brain injury he suffered due to a gang beating. I waved his picture in the air along with many others asking for and believing in healing of their loved ones who couldn't be there.

I remember when I was a teenager, my father used to always watch Pastor Benny and even send money to him. My dad was a disabled veteran and very sick. He believed that Pastor Benny would intercede on his behalf and help him be healed. I used to make jokes about Pastor Benny because back then it really looked phony to me. I thought it was crazy how canes and wheelchairs were thrown down off the stage. My dad commanded me to stop. My father really believed in his ministry. He was a single parent raising my brother and me. And he died watching Pastor Benny and others like him on Christian TV. I thought, *if my dad could see me now, he would be proud to see me dealing with these folks.*

So the service went on and since our church was a hosting church, a lot of the staff from FCC was in the VIP section too. Pastor Benny acknowledged some of the pastors towards the end of the service. Pastor Munsey was on the stage with him, so I felt honored and highly favored to be there and invited by Benny Hinn's daughter.

The service ended and as I walked out of the building I was on cloud nine. But once I saw people leaving in wheelchairs crying, and saw that the very sickly had not been healed, I began to feel very sad. I wondered, *what is this?* People had such hope and gave their money in the offering while holding on to their faith and expecting to be healed. My heart broke. *They will be healed in God's timing,* I thought.

After the crusade, the people in leadership at FCC began treating me differently. People would come up to me in the hallways and sanctuary of the church and prophesy and tell me how the hand of God and His favor were on my life. I was just overwhelmed that people had great things to say to me all the time! I never had such positivity in my life. To experience people loving on me and accepting me was a huge deal for me. It meant the world. I seemed to finally be in a place where I was accepted, even though I knew deep down that it wasn't about me.

I loved FCC. I would even go there when they were closed at night to pray outside the building, where there was a cross out front. Sometimes I would go pray on the altar in the empty sanctuary just to be in the building. I truly wanted to understand, grasp, and put into reality what Pastor Munsey was teaching me.

Even though I had gotten a lot of attention, I still was extremely lonely and poor. I was living far below the poverty line. Jobs were scarce at the time in the Chicago area. I would become discouraged at times.

It was late spring of 2005, over a year had passed since I was at FCC and all of those things that I was naming and claiming were not yet mine. I started to feel that maybe I was not doing something right. I was starting to feel like I couldn't go on in this lifestyle of lack, and I was hearing at Bible studies and on Sundays that I was the one who possibly wasn't doing something right because of my poverty. I had faith, sown seed and was encouraged each time I went to church, yet I knew that my time there was coming to an end.

I started to feel like my future in ministry was somewhere else. I was feeling a tugging to leave. I had to quit culinary school because of my financial situation. I even asked the church if I could have a job at the Starbucks since they were hiring, but they told me I hadn't volunteered long enough.

I had been looking for work for a long time, and nothing was happening. But one day, a prophetess at the church, whose son ran a ministry I was a part of that catered to 20-30 year olds at FCC, prophesied and told me that I would work for Benny Hinn. I received her prophesy and she actually kept pressing the issue every time that I saw her. She would say that I would be in California very soon. She had been at the church when Jessica and Michael had visited before, and she told me that she could see that they loved me. After we initially met, I had seen Jessica and Michael a few more times when they came to town to visit FCC because their family was close to Pastor Munsey and his family.

After a year and a few months at FCC it was time to go. My season had run its course. I wanted to do more for the Lord. I didn't know if I would work for the televangelist, but I did realize that there was more in store for me. I had lived in California before, and considered going back. Jessica and her fiancé Michael came to visit our church again and this particular time when we talked, she told me all about the church they were starting under her father's ministry, and she told me if I moved to California that I should come to their church.

To me this was confirmation that it was definitely time to leave Illinois and move back to California. I was excited, and I began to make plans to move to Orange County, California. I told Pastor Munsey that I was moving. He had been my spiritual father and teacher, and I definitely wanted his blessing before I left. He prayed for me and told me to go to his brother's church in Mission Viejo, CA.

I informed the other ministry at FCC that I was a part of that I was leaving. The Pastor and his mother, the one who had prophesied that I was going were extremely excited for me. They sent me off with a few dollars for which I was very grateful. I gave away pretty much everything in the house, put what I needed in my car and shipped my little red Chevy Aveo to California. My son and I went to Midway Airport in Chicago, boarded the plane, and were on to our next mission.

Orange County was beautiful! A new start began with a 700 square ft. two-bedroom one-bath condo. I was able to afford it with my government Section 8 housing. I also had to apply for the same help with food stamps and other assistance. Nevertheless, I was determined that life would be better here, somehow. I was quite happy with the condo, and thanked God I didn't have to pay market rent rates. I felt blessed to be able to participate in the government assisted program. My son had a safe place to stay, and he was going to school in one of the best school districts in the country. They had even named the town I moved to, Irvine, CA the safest city in America that year, so we were off to a grand start.

I was only a few minutes from where Benny Hinn's World Healing Center Church (WHCC) was with Pastor Michael Koulianos and the now Jessica Hinn-Koulianos. Now, Pastor Munsey had told me to visit his brother's church which was only a few minutes away in Mission Viejo, CA and I did at first … but ultimately, I chose WHCC.

It was a cute little wedding chapel on a campground in San Juan Capistrano, CA, from which I understood was owned by Pastor Robert Shuller of the Crystal Cathedral Church in Garden Grove, Ca. He was letting WHCC use the chapel to hold churh services in the late afternoons because that was the only time it was available on Sundays due to weddings taking place.Pastor Benny gave his son in law charge over WHCC and Pastor Benny was listed as the senior pastor. It was a new ministry in its beginning stages. I felt that my son and I could grow there with new fresh eyes and a fresh anointing. There was a new move going on: all of the pastors and co-pastors were young, and I admired their zeal and vision. I was ready and willing to help in every way possible. I wanted to be a servant of the Lord and make myself available to God.

I got special recognition in the church because of Jessica and Michael's close relationship with Pastor Munsey. I began to serve wholeheartedly and volunteer for various works such as the children's ministry and community events like a carnival we put on free of charge for the community. I would sit with the elderly and disabled until their bus picked them up after church services, or I would give them rides home. My son and I were at the church every time the doors opened, ready to help and wanting to be in the will of God. But I was still looking for work, and Pastor Michael and Jessica were aware of that.

One night I had a dream that Pastor Benny died! In my dream I was watching the news, which showed pictures of him from the time he was young until the time of his current age. All around the world people were commenting; some were crying, and some were shocked. I didn't know what happened to him. I just remembered people saying things from all over the world in different languages and nationalities. I did not know what this dream meant.

It felt extremely weird, and when I woke up, I was crying as if the dream was real. I went to church that evening and brought my cousin Virniecia with me as a guest. She lived in Riverside County and was also a follower of Pastor Benny — she was excited and wanted to check out the church.

I had been bragging about my new Pastor Michael and my new friend Jessica. I was compelled to talk to Michael and Jessica about my dream after service but before I could get to them Jessica approached me and asked me if I would be willing to go into her father's home to work for her family. I was floored, needless to say. She began to go on and say that she knew that it was not much but they felt that they could trust me in the house. She told me to think about it.

I dropped to my knees in awe, right in the sanctuary. I was crying, as I was realizing the prophecy over my life. I was overwhelmed and humbled by the request! The dream I had the night prior stumped me. What could it mean? How were the two connected?

With everything to lose, I went to a known prophetess and friend to the Hinn family who was in the service that night, and I explained what I dreamed and told her about the position. She asked me if the dream was in black and white or color. I told her color. She said if it was in color then that meant that the dream was not demonic. She laid her hands on my head and prayed and prophesied over me like I had never been prayed or prophesied over before. I was crying tears of joy, feeling as though I were the chosen one. I thought *what an honor it is to serve the man of God and his family*!

I went to tour the parsonage the next day, and I was totally amazed. I had never seen such a gorgeous home in my life, a home that overlooked the ocean. The furnishings, high ceilings, staircase and beautiful custom flooring! So extravagant, I felt as if I were dreaming. And speaking of dreaming, when I walked down one of the hallways in the home, there were pictures that closely resembled the ones I had seen in my dream of Pastor Benny. It was too much for me to comprehend, because I had never been in this home before …. I felt that this was God doing something supernatural in my life.

I accepted the position to work at the parsonage. I also got offered the opportunity to work at the studio in Aliso Viejo, helping to prep the set for Pastor Benny's television show "This is Your Day" and making sure that everything in his office and greenroom was perfect for him. This was a journey I was ready to begin.

Pastor Michael and Jessica Hinn-Koulianos

Dear Friends,

It is with deepest humility that Jessica and I share our hearts with you today. Our father, Pastor Benny, has entrusted us with the honor and privilege of shepherding the flock of World Healing Center Church. For this privilege we will be eternally grateful to him. We are humbled by this calling of God, and by His grace we pledge ourselves to faithfully fulfill this most important role of pastoring His precious saints.

Our prayer is that the love of Christ Jesus will always be the center of all we do and say. In the Spirit of the Lord's love, we trust that He will strengthen and anoint each of us in order to fulfill His divine summons. We are here for you and want you to know that we come as servants to wash your feet and feed His lambs. With your prayers and support, united in one vision, we will see souls saved and the sick healed, all in the name of Jesus.

Please know that Jessica and I long to live lives that will allow us to hear from God so we may share His Word with you. As your pastor, I pray that the Lord's will be done.

In Christ's Service.

World Healing Center Church
Rancho Capistano
29251 Camino Capistrano
San Juan Capistrano, CA 92675

WORLD HEALING CENTER CHURCH

PASTOR MICHAEL & MRS. JESSICA KOULIANOS

WHCC brochure

OUR
Vision:

1. Exemplify the *Love of Christ* (Ephesians 5:19)

2. Always surrender to the leading of the *Holy Spirit* (1 Thessalonians 5:19)

3. Focus on *Evangelism* to bring the lost to Christ (Matthew 10:6)

4. *Worship* in Spirit and in Truth. (John 4:24)

5. *Engage the Saints* for ministry. (2 Timothy 4:12)

6. *Outreach* to the hurting in our community. (James 1:27)

7. Preach the *Word of God* with boldness. (Romans 10:8)

8. *Support* the Christ-centered family unit. (1 Timothy 5:8)

9. Minister to the *Youth and Children* of our church body. (1 Timothy 4:12)

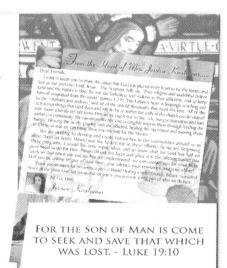

FOR THE SON OF MAN IS COME TO SEEK AND SAVE THAT WHICH WAS LOST. – LUKE 19:10

WHCC brochure

June 28, 2005

Dear Jessica,

I pray that you and Pastor Michael are having a blessed day. I wanted to write to you to let you know how much you'll have been a blessing to me. The first time we met in Chicago I knew that it was totally of God. That day I made myself get up out of bed. I had been battling with depression. I had rededicated my life to the Lord and I went to church thinking I was going to find a new members class I also had my spice blend I developed in my hand hoping I would network with some people so that I could go out like kernal sanders! But they didn't have a class that day and someone asked me if I could come help feed the homeless. I was happy to be able to help, I was a culinary arts student,I love serving others, plus I've been homeless a few times in my 29 years. But I know that the Lord wanted to give me hope and peace that day. And he wanted me to feel the power of God in a way that I never had before and receive healing. When you and pastor michael prayed with me that day I felt so much love it was the spirit of God. I was numb for a few hours trying to understand me? Little old me Lord? me out of everyone else that needed help out there that day. He guided you guys towards me right on time. Praise the Lord! I have had so much peace lately. I had suffered from anxiety attacks and cried every night for almost five years straight. I had migraines for as long as I could remember and hearing problems from my right ear from some form of violence. One thing I now understand that pastor Steve Munsey has taught me is to never break your rank' I never would have imaged that in the midst of all hell breaking loose I could still have peace and joy knowing that the Lord is the only truth and the only light that he knows what he is doing in our lives and why. If I had wallowed in my sorrows that day I would have probably never met you guys. I definitely would not have gotton VIP seats for the crusade! And I thank the Lord everyday for his devine appointments. It feels soooo good to not have a migraine, it feels wonderful to be able to hear clearly out of my right ear, It's been almost a year now .My father used to watch your father. I used to not believe. I used to laugh. But the Lord knew the hour that I would praise him at a Benny Hinn crusade and receive healing. I stand in amazement everyday of what the Lord has done and is doing in my life and I give him all the praise. I'm learning how to totally trust him, love him, depend on him, he is my everything! Jesus is all I've ever needed. I thank you for being a true sister and brother in the Lord. Great things are going to happen with your ministry because you'll are keeping it real. I know that it is a great responsibility and everything is not peachy. The Lord always gives us strength right in the nick of time. I recently read the books of Zephaniah and I have no words to describe how I felt. Only that the people need to hear it. I wanted to leave you with Psalms 121 and let you know that if there is anything that I could do to help I'm there, me and my, son he's only 6 but he needs a job.

God Bess You
Cheryl Brown

Dear Jessica letter from me

2

SACRIFICIAL GIVING

WHCC was a non-denominational church with a charismatic, healing, prophetic, prosperity twist. When I was there, I learned a lot about the concept of sacrificial giving as I did at FCC. Pastor Michael was my new pastor. He was a couple of years younger than me and he seemed very nice. He was pretty much in control of every aspect of the church service. His church attendees knew exactly when to give God praise, give God money, and when to sit down. There wasn't a lot of hopping around and being out of order at WHCC — it was extremely organized and structured. Security was also very tight. His main security guard was a huge Samoan guy named Lungo, who was like a gentle giant to everyone.

Under the code of sacrificial giving, I gave everything that I could: my time, my heart and soul, and even my last few dollars. I believed in the ministry with my entire being, and I was so excited for my son and I to be accepted there. I was called upon often to come up in front of the church to speak or to testify. I was very poor financially, yet I had victory in Jesus!

I also knew how to deal with the people that were coming into the ministry, especially the poor ones. I knew that God was taking me to a different destination in life to advance his kingdom. All that I had ever endured in this life was because he was preparing me for this ministry. This was very serious, not only was I serving a man of God on the forefront of ministry, but I was under the umbrella of the entire family. I was being equipped for ministry "for such a time as this," as I was told.

I felt that there was something great that would come out of this whole situation from the start. Pastor Michael and Jessica came from such a powerful teacher as Pastor Benny that I gave them great credit without a second thought. Besides, they had been so nice to me. When it was offering time, I was a cheerful giver. Sometimes I didn't know how my son and I were going to make it financially, but we always seemed to. My son was even excited to give his last bit of change.

They taught heavily about the woman in the Bible who gave the little that she had and how she was honored more than the rich man, who gave plenty, because of her sacrificing. She was blessed abundantly. So I gave, and when I ran out of money, I would give my jewelry, and when I ran out of jewelry I gave more of my time. I was always willing to give my time.

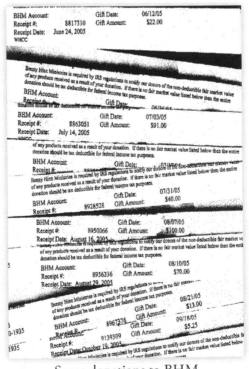

Some donations to BHM

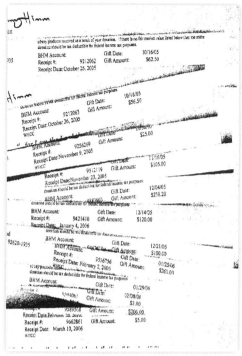

Sacrificial giving

Dear Cheryl,

Thank you so much for attending WHCC. We pray God's best for you in each and every area of your life.

Thank you for coming and serving in the House of the Lord — and we pray you continue to grow and flourish as you are living and giving in His presence.

God Bless You,
Pastor Michael & Jessica

A thank you card from Jessica & Pastor Michael

A lot of the people who came to the church had relocated from other cities and countries because they believed that they were called to be a part of Pastor Benny's ministry. They packed up and came down on faith without anything! Not even a place to stay. They always thought that they would see Pastor Benny at a service, but he was never present.

I had begun to see that Pastor Michael was having a very hard time relating to his poor church members. I remember having a conversation with Jessica once, and she told me that she was born with a silver spoon in her mouth and that she did not know how it felt to have to go without anything. To me that was truth, and I really appreciated that from her.

They knew that I had extensive experiences with hard times, so I became a sort of mediator of social services to the members. I remember one particular family with four children moved to the area because of the church, and they needed help with food. Pastor Michael helped them out once, but when they came a second time he complained. In his fury one day he asked how they could come here with nothing?

A lot of the members would use their last amount of gas just to get to church. I found it amazing that they went beyond their comfort zone to reach for something more than what they had, even if it was just another church service. I explained to Pastor Michael that because they stepped out on faith, they believed that God would supernaturally provide for them. This was what they taught us, after all. He seemed disturbed, and said that his help was limited.

I knew that just from being a single mother that it is hard to reach out sometimes. And if you are a man reaching out for your family, that must be even harder. But I believe that God's help is not limited, and if he helped us once, he would help us again and again. I believe that Our God is not a God who would turn us away. I felt that as cheerfully as poor members of the church gave their last, the pastor should be equally cheerful giving back to them.

I would see Pastor Michael after church being escorted out by his security. He would even wave goodnight to my son and me as I carried bags and an elderly woman on my arm trying to make it to my car without dropping anything. Sometimes I would think to myself, *how could he be a young man with security, hands free and not even offer a hand to help me or the elderly? Even my son knew better than that!*

There was a continual flow of poor people coming through the doors of WHCC. Not only were they poor, they were sick, physically and mentally. Pastor Michael did not know how to handle this. When the people would begin to share with each other and state their concerns to Pastor Michael, he would get upset. One of the things that he would always say in his sermons was, "I can point you in two directions, to Jesus or to the exit sign!" I believe that Pastor Michael thought originally that all the rich people in Orange County would come to WHCC.

Things became very interesting; many of the people that came were Benny Hinn fanatics, freaks, and worshippers. Once some of the members caught onto the fact that I was in the parsonage, they would try to cling to me. I even had some people at the church and Benny Hinn Ministry staffs ask me to lay my hands on them and pray for them. I didn't do it. People that had worked in the ministry for several years would say how the favor of the Lord was on me and how it was such an honor for me to be in his house.

A couple of the staff at the studio asked if I could come and clean their homes, and I would do it for literally nothing. They were very curious about who Cheryl was. They also would tell me about how I should be careful to treat all of the Hinns like royalty. They told me that as long as I remembered that it was all about them, that I would be OK. I listened, but didn't respond much. I am from Chicago, and I know the saying about gossip that "if a dog will bring a bone, a dog will carry one," so I took it all in stride. I even remember being so devoted to WHCC and the Hinn's that at times I would get offended at some of the things I would hear.

They told me how Pastor Hinn pays the entire ministry peanuts and how they had all relocated to be with him, and how they had sacrificed their entire lives for the ministry. They told me how they were barely making ends meet themselves, and how they were even behind on their rent for their apartments. They were curious to know what I was getting paid. I didn't mind, I told them, and they told me that they wished that they could afford to have me help them at their places more often. I went to clean Benny's mom's condo once she moved; it was located a few minutes away from the parsonage. Pastor Michael even had me come to clean his home once, which was beautiful as well. I was on call and would never be sure what I would be called for but I was always ready to braid hair, run errands, cook and clean, etc. Even though it was a lot of physically demanding work, it gave me a sense of belonging and I wanted to show my dedication.

A couple of months into working for the Hinns, two devastating events happened within a few days of each other. One was Hurricane Katrina. I was so devastated and my heart was there, and I wanted to go to help. I thought that the ministry would go but I don't remember that happening. To me that was where Benny Hinn needed to be in his "calling." Running through some hospitals and disaster sites.

Then, I got a call that my niece was killed in a car accident and I was in shock! I was in pieces; I asked an insider if they thought I could go to the funeral. I didn't think that they would have a problem with it. But they actually came back and told me "no," that if I left I may not have a job when I return.

Now I pondered this and I know that everyone has certain ways to deal with things … I knew I didn't have the money to go anyway. Since they suggested that I don't go, I definitely didn't think they would help me with a ticket. So, disappointed and grieving, I continued to go to work at Pastor Benny's home.

There was nothing worse than being so poor that when someone dies you don't have money for a ticket. Also it raised a flag when they said I might not have a job if I left to go to my 11-year-old niece's funeral. As much as I had worked in ministry, the poverty was paralyzing as ever and yet I still continued to give what I could, knowing that my breakthrough was on the way.

I would see the older disabled ladies waiting on their buses to arrive after service, and they would be there alone. Everyone else in the church would have left and not helped them until there was only my son and I left. The picture was a single parent waiting with these elderly disabled ladies to make sure that they were safely on the bus at night. Sometimes younger ladies would come as well, poor and living in shelters. I would make sure they had a meal and sleeping bags as I took them to their shelters. After a while I realized how little concern there was for these poor people. Things started to not feel so right.

I eventually spoke to Jessica about how I was only getting paid 10 bucks an hour and how I could hardly make ends meet myself. I knew that it was an honor to work for the Hinn's, yet I was a single mother and I planned on living better than I had been in Illinois. She said that she would speak to her parents about it. I was happy, because a part of me wanted to know if they really cared about the wellbeing of my son and me.

But the next service after I spoke to Jessica, Pastor Michael looked directly at me while he was preaching and stated that "the Red Sea has been parted for you, now you need to do the rest." He acted very cold towards me after service, and I guess it was because of me stating my circumstances to Jessica.

I knew that it was a ministry and I was so grateful to be able to work at the parsonage, but I discovered that they were paying me a rate based on what Texans get paid, because the headquarters were in Texas. I did not feel it was just. I was in Orange County, California, where I found out that people in my position got paid over three times the amount I made. I was concerned, and had hoped for a little something more. I never heard anything else about the pay from Jessica, but I remained diligent and continued to serve Pastor Benny and his family. I felt that I was put there to pray, and, maybe I would receive tips eventually?

Sometimes Mrs. Hinn would give me the old food out of the fridge to take home. It would be old milk, fruits, and cooked food that didn't smell too well. She would just get a bag and say, "Here, you can have all of this," like I wanted it. It wasn't fit for her dog to eat, yet I took it because I didn't want to dare act like I was somebody. I felt that we were getting closer by her giving me the ribs that they had eaten from probably a week prior. Although I had grown wary of my surroundings, I was still very excited about what was to come. I would pray and thought that I could only go up from here.

I would see Jessica and Pastor Michael at the parsonage sometimes. One day she told me that she was getting rid of some things and wanted to know if I could use them. I was happy that she thought of me. Jessica even had Lungo come to my place and bring me a coffee table, futon, and big huge box of their belongings.

My son and I were starting over fresh, so these items were a blessing to us. The things were all thrown in the box any kind of way, like rubbish, but one man's trash is another man's treasure. I was picking through this stuff like a bum in an ally dumpster, just sorting through. One sock was entangled with Pastor Michael's underwear and Jessica's broken jewelry, along with worn old pantyhose, etc. But there were also lots of nice things in it as well: purses, belts, clothes, and shoes.

I was digging through the box and there were Jessica's wedding shoes. When I got to church, I told her, "Girl, I have your wedding shoes!" But she told me that she wanted me to keep them to wear when I got married. We wore the same size shoe. I was honored. She told me that they would have more things to give me because they were getting rid of stuff while they settled into their new home. I was very grateful for what they had done but I refused to accept anything else, because after finally going through this huge box, there was a DVD with a man in some tiger underwear sitting in a casket with the name Steve-O on it! Who was this? Some sort of porn star? I actually viewed some of the content. I wanted to see what the shepherds over my soul were into? It totally sickened me. I was appalled at what I saw; it consisted of pornography, profanity and extreme grossness to say the least.

I never told them that they had left it in the box, and I threw it in the garbage along with some other offensive things. I was trying my best to live a pure and Christian lifestyle, and I didn't want that filth in my home or my spirit, and I was very disappointed. I continued to pray for my young pastors. Clearly a lot of things were happening within this ministry that was not OK.

But why would I stay, some may ask? The real question for me was, why would I go? If God had placed me there, I was not supposed to leave. I thought that maybe I was there to try to help make it better. It had become clear to me that I was on some type of assignment. I began to pray and serve them even harder.

Obviously these young pastors didn't have a clue of what it was like to be poor or needy, and they didn't have a clue of what it meant to work toward having expensive things, and it was extremely alarming, because they had a lot of control over people's lives. People would stand in line just to shake Michael and Jessica's hands because they just wanted some of that "anointing that they thought would rub off on them". People desired to be healed, delivered, set free, rich and saved by the Benny Hinn Ministries.

Now, WHCC consisted of 100-200 members on a good day. And sometimes Pastor Michael would not even stand there to greet a few people that had been waiting in line to see him. He would vanish with his security and leave one of his co-pastors to handle the rest. I saw that once he married Jessica and they had their first child, he had become exceedingly arrogant. Family and staff that had started out with WHCC started leaving the church and relocating elsewhere. I never got into all that was going on, but I knew that some of members were extremely upset. I began to wonder about the arrangement, was it all about keeping it in the family or just business? I remember Pastor Michael saying that he didn't advertise much because of who the Hinn's were. That he knew that people would only want to come because of them. WHCC members were told that they were the chosen ones. I was disenchanted with a multitude of things I saw and heard, yet I stayed put.

World Healing Center Church

Requests the honor of your
presence
this Sunday
the eleventh of September
two thousand five
At four thirty in the afternoon

Rancho Capistrano
29251 Camino Capistrano
In San Juan Capistrano, California

Fellowship and refreshments will be
provided as well as a special gift
from
Pastor Michael and Mrs. Jessica
Koulianos

WHCC special service

3

IN THE PARSONAGE

I knew that I was on the verge of a breakthrough, and that God had a plan for my son and me to prosper spiritually and financially. So in the midst of my ugly, increasingly dire financial situation, I now was working in the parsonage (I was taught to address the house only as the parsonage) for Pastor Benny. The favor of the Lord was upon me!

I took great pleasure in going to work; it was a beautiful drive. Here I was in my little cherry red Chevy Aveo driving to Dana Point, California. Every morning I would turn on my praise and worship music to adore the Lord and pray as I drove in to work. I thanked the Lord for a job, and I thanked the Lord for His favor on my life. I knew it was not a coincidence that I was in this position. Even if it just consisted of cleaning toilets and doing laundry, it was a great start, and it was helping to serve the man of God.

Benny Hinn's parsonage was quite the ritzy place. The Ritz Carlton and Salt Creek Beach was right next to the gated community. It definitely felt amazingly incredible driving up to an over 10 million dollar home overlooking the Pacific Ocean. The views were magnificent and everything was fancy to say the least. I believe the parsonage was at least a good 8000 square feet.

I had worked at the parsonage for three days before I ever met Pastor Benny up close and personal. I was very anxious to meet him and when I was finally called up those stairs from that laundry room, I thought that when he first met me that I would be slain in the spirit just like what happens at the Miracle Crusades! But that didn't happen at all. Instead, we shook hands and he asked me a few questions. One question I remembered him asking me was "Cheryl, how old are you? " I said 29, and he said that I looked 19. That was quite the compliment. Flattered, I thanked him, smiled and swiftly went back to work. Those three days of waiting to meet him had me on eggshells.

When I started working for Pastor Benny, I found that my pay would only be 10 dollars an hour. I was still on government housing and food stamps, yet I knew that God was putting me in a position to advance the kingdom. My goal was to be able to quickly work my way up the ranks and be able to get off of government assistance.

I felt very privileged to be able to go to work for them. I was in the man's home, after all, and it was a great feeling. I laughed to myself sometimes like, "Wow! My father would just be tickled to see me here." I drove up to Dana Point every morning with pride in my heart. I drove into the gated community with my monthly pass proudly displayed on my car window, and I entered a special code to enter through the garage, where I really got a load of the fleet of Mercedes Benzes that were in the garage. Every car and truck that was there was a Benz. Even the dog's name was Mercedes. *Now this was prosperity!*

Sometimes I would have to sweep and mop the garage floors to keep them shining and squeaky clean. When "the man" was coming back into town, I was taught to get everything super perfect for the grand entry, just like he was a king. When he came home he typically came through the garage and passed down the hall by the laundry room. When he strolled through, he would wave at me, hands free, with his security behind him carrying his large collection of Louis Vuitton luggage. I made sure that the rug was down and vacuumed.

The laundry room was one of the areas where I spent a lot of time. It was tiny, consisting of cabinets, counters, a washer and dryer, irons, starch, and ironing boards. Sometimes there would be two of us there, Sue and I. Sue was my teacher. She had been with the Hinn family for at least 13 years. Her husband was his butler/everything man.

Sue taught me everything I needed to know about how exactly Pastor Benny wanted things done in the house and at the studio. She was a great woman. I learned a lot of tricks from her about their very special way of cleaning, and appreciated everything she taught me. When I came, she was happy that I was there to help. I asked her if I could bring a small radio for the laundry area and a little picture of my son and she said I could. She and I would do laundry for hours in that little room, and we needed a little entertainment. I brought in this tiny radio and we would be listening to the latest Christian music with the volume down very low. It put pep in our step and Sue would tell me how she really enjoyed working with me.

People that worked in the parsonage with the Hinn's for years called me a jewel. Things were going great. I was working hard and feeling good about it. From the time that Pastor Benny and his family stepped out of the shower, finished eating, and threw their dirty clothes down the chute, I was there to clean the shower, clean the kitchen, and wash, dry, iron, fold and put up the clothing.

I had a procedure that allowed me to be "quietly efficient." My goal was to never disturb Pastor Benny. There were three levels of the home. If he was eating, I would go clean his bedroom or work upstairs. If he was resting I would go in the kitchen or sweep the outside of the home or continue to work on clothing downstairs. In other words, unless he was requesting something, I was invisible.

He did not want to see the broom, mop, rags, or anything else we used for cleaning. When cleaning any area of the home, I would have to place my tools out of view in a closet. It was a rule.

I was told that having these things visible would interfere with his anointing. I would have to vacuum his rugs in his bedroom a certain way because he did not want to see zigzags on the carpet. I would lift the vacuum with each stroke and pull it backward, because he wanted it all straight! I would have to use a rug comb to make sure the fringes on the exotic rugs were perfect in the living area. His pillows also had to be perfectly aligned on his bed, and there were a lot of them, all in the colors of rich reds and royal purples. And I would make a special solution of natural ingredients for cleaning his bathroom because he did not like the smell of chemicals. He could have been allergic to them like me.

For Pastor Benny there were definitely several special requirements. I remember one time I had to have had at least 50 Versace shirts of every color of the rainbow—yellow, peach, purple, coral, etc.—all starched and ironed. *Very flamboyant*, I thought. I later heard that his name is in a famous designer's store window alongside the names of other elite people.

Another requirement was that all of his slacks be steam pressed (instead of sending out to a drycleaners). One time I accidentally burned a pair of his black Versace pants with the iron; it looked like caramel had spilled on them, they were sizzling. I was so nervous. Thank goodness he had several duplicates of the same pants. It was not my fault though, the irons we had were not commercial quality and had simply overheated. I heard that he laughed and thought it was funny. That put my mind at ease and I was so happy it didn't have to come out of my check. I was only getting paid ten dollars an hour, and who knew how much those Versace pants cost.

I eventually heard that he loved my ironing, so once the ministry bought another iron, from that point on I was an ironing machine. I even ironed his socks, his underwear, his towels, and his handkerchiefs. There was a special folding and pressing technique I had to learn from Sue for his underwear and handkerchiefs.

After everything in the laundry department was cleaned, folded, and pressed, the clothing had to be put in drawers or hung in closets. The last thing that you would want to see was something clean coming back down the chute. I started seeing socks and undershirts come back down. I would ask Sue why, and she would say "Oh, maybe one sock was a little longer than the other," or "Maybe he didn't like the way the T-shirt was folded." I was being held to a very high standard. I was seeing just what it meant to work for a king.

A lot of times I would clean the entire house by myself. One time I actually saved Pastor Benny from getting seriously hurt or worse. I had just finished mopping the staircase and here he comes running light on his feet from his room, about to run down the staircase, and I shouted, "Pastor no, it's wet!" He abruptly stopped, held onto the rail, walked down the stairs slowly, and said, "Touch that back up for me." I did, relieved that he had not slipped. I don't know what I would have done if he would have fallen down those stairs.

Now I was new and I recognized that I was there to answer their every need, yet there was a certain task that thoroughly disgusted me, because common courtesy goes a long way. The first or second time I overlooked it, but after a while I started to wonder if the females in the home knew how to flush the toilet. Yes, this was a nerve wrecker to me! There were ten bathrooms, and this was happening almost daily in a few of them. I had to deal with the fact that someone's crap stared me in the face almost every day and not only did I have to be the one to flush it, but sometimes I had to become a plumber in the situation. I thought that this behavior was not only lazy, but disrespectful of themselves and the people who worked in the house! I was just not getting paid enough. *Isn't cleanliness next to Godliness?* I thought.

For Mrs. Hinn I was an emotional outlet for her to vent, a prayer partner, and buddy when she needed one. We even developed a system to weed out offensive clothing that was coming down the chute. I would go and sort laundry only to find "obscenities" on it. There were so many sexually explicit and drug related items coming down that chute that it got to the point of me having to speak to Mrs. Hinn. I was totally offended.

We came up with the system where I collect and bag the offensive things and give them to her, and she would then give them to Pastor Benny. I was happy with that arrangement, but a few days later it would be right back in my face. I would let Mrs. Hinn know and one time she put me on the phone with Pastor Benny about it. I was really embarrassed. She had me tell him what was on the sexually explicit clothing only.

She assured me that it all would stop. But after that conversation, as I walked out of the room, I could pretty much hear her say to him that it wasn't funny and saying that he shouldn't have a 'boys would be boys" attitude about this. I felt pretty disrespected to see the clothes come back once again after I had talked to him about them. It made me feel confused. I felt like there was no regard for me as a woman. I *did* ask her that if I saw things that were offensive again could I just throw them out, and she told me no, that if I did that I may lose my job. I simply said OK. Insulted, I left that situation alone.

Mrs. Hinn was a shopaholic, whenever she would return from a shopping spree; I would run to her to grab her bags so she didn't have to carry them. She had a beautiful tall jewelry chest full of jewelry. The woman had purses and clothing spilling out of her closet like a hoarder. She had tons of clothing and shoes in her closet that she had not even worn. One time I looked at the price tag of an undergarment, and it cost more than what I got paid in a week.

I would also have to check and empty her clothing pockets before I would wash them. I was very honest and every dime I found I would place on her vanity. I would always find money, wads of it, in her jeans. The money would be from other countries; just a lot of it balled up in several bunches, like there was no regard for it! I was there barely making ends meet and to see such carelessness was honestly sickening. I did like Mrs. Hinn, but I did not understand the way she interacted with me. It was as if

she were a yoyo, one day she was up up up and the next well?!
Your guess is as good as mine. It was impossible to know what to
expect from her.

One time I was in the home and I thought I was there alone;
I always worked in the same manner, whether I was alone or not,
because I was working unto the Lord. So, there I was working
hard and sure enough someone came up behind me. It was Pastor
Benny. I was glad that my Chicago reflex didn't set in and I didn't
drop kick him! He handed me 300 bucks in cash and told me not
to tell anyone. I thanked him, and God knows that it was on time!
I was hoping that this would happen more often.

I would always make sure things were perfect for him and add
little touches to make sure he was happy. For example, he loved to
see fruit on the counter in the kitchen, pineapples, oranges, etc.
and we had to pick the best. One time I went to the local Gelson's
to pick oranges and it was $4 per orange! *It must be nice,* I thought.
I would dust the beautiful white piano keys and clean the exotic
fish tank that went from the floor to the ceiling. I would love to
go walk out on the grounds and feel the breeze off the ocean as I
swept the leaves and debris off the patio area. I couldn't help but
to pause a second and revel in the luxury.

The balcony view off the Hinn's bedroom was breathtaking
and stunning as well! I loved to go onto the balcony of the prayer
room too, I used to go in there and clean the outside windows of
the balcony. I would have to stand on a chair to clean them and
to dust the ceiling fans. I had heard that a lot of the great men of
God had been there in the prayer room, such as Oral Roberts and
even my former Pastor Steve Munsey. I would pray most of the
time when I was at the parsonage while I was working. When I
didn't really understand my plight, I knew that God was watching
over me.

I remember one day Pastor Benny was preparing to travel out
of the country, and Mrs. Hinn had instructed me to not put the
pillows on their bed when I went up to clean their bedroom. As I
was finishing, His security came up, placed his suitcase on the bed

and began packing his things. I exited the room and no more than a couple of minutes later, there Pastor Benny was yelling "Cheryl!" in a loud, stern voice. "Why aren't my pillows on the bed?" he roared angrily. Shaking, I stated to him that Mrs. Hinn instructed me not to put them on, and he yelled, "This is my house and I want the pillows on the bed!" I said "Yes sir!" to him and ran to put those pillows on the bed immediately. The security guard just shook his head. I mean, obviously since he was leaving Mrs. Hinn felt like she didn't want the pillows, and it was such a small detail. For him to become irate about that was startling.

I began to see just how vain and self-absorbed this man was. He even used Dove soap to bathe in, and there were stacks of it in the closets. A dove was his signature symbol; the emblem of a dove was on all his suits. And when we got those suits back from the cleaners we had to hang all of them in his glass closet he had built especially for them.

I went from being called "Darling" to "Cheryl" to" ay" in a matter of weeks, and my workload was getting heavier than ever. I even had to walk and play with the dog Mercedes, and they knew I was terrified of dogs. I was told I would have to conquer that fear if I was going to be there, and miraculously, I did.

I walked the dog and played catch with her. She was a black Labrador retriever, and very smart. I had never been this close to a dog before. One time Mrs. Hinn said that the dog really liked me. She said that dogs were very spiritual and they can read people. For some strange reason I felt totally accepted into Mrs. Hinn's world because the dog liked me. One time this dog was around me so much as I was grieving for my niece, and she just came up to me and started rubbing her head on my knees. I was in the kitchen pantry organizing and I just started crying. When I came out, Mrs. Hinn just came up to me and gave me a hug. I apologized for crying and told her about my niece and she told me that the dog felt my pain.

One day I was at the parsonage alone, wiping down the kitchen counters, and I had a vision that the entire home flooded. In my vision, water rushed into the home from the ocean and the home was destroyed. I could not stop thinking about this vision. I didn't know what it meant. After I had the vision I went over to one of the living areas to sit for a moment because I was overwhelmed and a bit uneasy from this vision. As I sat, my eyes gazed towards a book on the coffee table about Kathryn Kuhlman. I later found out that she was the lady who inspired his ministry. I saw a video of her and I noticed the similarities between her and Pastor Benny. It also reminded me of how Pastor Michael at services would mimic Pastor Benny with his tone, pitch, and body movements. Now that I think about it, it was almost like he was a fake "mini Benny." I don't know what my vision meant or the connection to Kathryn Kuhlman, but I had to get back to work, as weird as it was, and think about this peculiar vision later.

When Pastor Benny was away there would be days where I would come in and Mrs. Hinn would tell me that I could leave. She just didn't want to be bothered. I know that it was hard for her to be his other half, but, Boy I tell you the crunch was on when it was time for him to return! My workload was a triple duty! I don't know what had happened when I was off, but it was horrible, to say the least. She absolutely did nothing in the home that I could see. I didn't blame him for having his own bathroom on the other side of their bedroom. He was, by far, the only neat freak there and he even gave a courtesy flush.

During the Christmas holidays, I, Sue, and a couple of other staff from BHM helped to put up and decorate the Christmas tree for Christmas of 2005 when they were out of town. He was gone to one place and she was in another. The tree was at least 12 feet tall. I had fun decorating the entire home and was really thrilled when they personally told me how much they loved it.

There was a built-in-sound system and I thought I would play some Christmas carols or gospel music as we were putting up the decorations, but it was already programmed! This song called" Rapper's Delight" came on. It was by this old school group called the "Sugar Hill Gang." When it started playing, I was uncontrollably cracking up with laughter. I was going to change it but I was informed by his more seasoned staffers that that was one of Benny Hinn's favorites. I was totally shocked as we were at the house jamming to the beat! It felt weird to know that this holy man listened to this type of music. I imagined him dancing around the house to it as well. Wow, comical, to say the least.

Anyway, it was finally Christmas day and I was only supposed to work from 8 in the morning until noon. My son was disappointed that I had to work that day, but he understood. I actually didn't mind going in for a few hours, however, I wound up not getting off until well after 5 PM. This was heartbreaking for me, just waiting around for their every call, as I watched them celebrate Christmas while I was away from my son. It took four hours for them to open gifts, after that I was prompted by Pastor Benny to clean a guest bathroom, right before I went in he told me that he was going to bless me financially. Apparently someone had just gone in and relieved him or herself and crap was everywhere! It was gross. I believed that someone had gotten high as a kite on Christmas day at the parsonage!

Pastor Benny told me he was going to bless me financially on Christmas, but he had told me that a few times before. All I wanted to do was go home; I knew that my baby was waiting on his mommy. I was so tired and a little down that day because I felt, by this time, that we would have been invited over for the holiday, not me having to work overtime.

About an hour later, I was finished cleaning the bathroom. I didn't have time to catch my breath before I was called into the kitchen to clean up after what they had been eating. I cleaned up all of the wrappings and garbage with a smile on my face as I continued to be made to order. One of his grown daughters was in the kitchen with him while I was cleaning; she dropped a stick of butter on the floor and before she could pick it up for herself, he asked me to pick it up. I did as quickly as he asked me but I thought, *Lord is this really happening to me right now?*

I knew that I was a maid, but this was becoming more direct, more degrading, more dehumanizing, and this was on the holiday that was all about giving. It was an especially hard time for me because my niece was killed in a car accident only a few months prior and my son was grieving as well. I just wanted to go home and be with my son. As much as I wanted to cry, I didn't have a second to think about it, because these folks were pulling and tugging on me to do this and that. When I finally left out of the door, there was a little basket on top of my car. *Awe,* I thought to myself, *someone had thought about little old me.* I cried and was happy to receive the basket. I felt relief as I finally picked my son up from a couple that worked in the ministry, because I couldn't find a sitter on Christmas.

When I arrived to pick up my son, I apologized to them for taking longer than I had originally thought. I did not even have a moment to call to let them know that I would be late. They were an older couple and their family was out of town so they told me that they didn't mind. They said, "Wow, you are surprised? We told you that it was all about them." I got their message, but still wondered why they had been in the ministry for so many years themselves. I just wanted to go home and get a shower. I was so happy to see my son. I grabbed him and we hugged each other, and we enjoyed what time we had left for the holiday.

Sometimes when I was on call on the weekends, I could bring my son with me. One time I went in to braid Benny Hinn's son's hair and Pastor Benny came down to watch me braid for a few minutes, and he met my son and spoke with him a bit. Everyone really enjoyed my son and sometimes Sue would pick sweet, clementine's off the tree out back for me to take to my son.

When we did a deep cleaning and would throw things out, Sue's husband would give us odd things like mugs from one of Pastor Benny's favorite shops, Harrods; empty gift baskets that had been sent to the family, or a license plate holder off one of the old Benzes. One time, Sue and her husband went to Jerusalem to serve Pastor Benny and brought a hat back for my son. I was told that one day I would get a chance to visit Jerusalem so I was looking forward to flying on the private jet! The Dove One is what I was hearing them call it. But in the meantime, when they left, it was my job to help ensure that things were smooth on the home front. I was told that I was doing a great work and that Pastor Benny could not do what he did in peace if we were not there to serve the man of God. I felt honored.

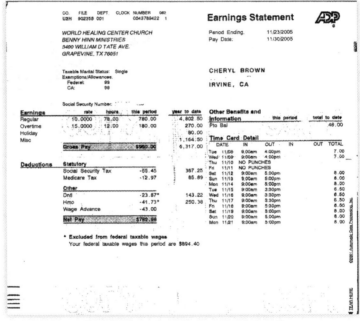

Paycheck stub and time card detail

"A DAY AT WORK WITH MOMMY"

Pastor Benny's street

Side view of parsonage

Driveway

In front of parsonage

Garage

The laundry room

The movie theater

The Jacuzzi/Patio area

4

I AM WATCHING YOU

I continued to be told that I was called and chosen by God to work in this ministry and in the parsonage. Even though things seemed odd at times, I knew that greatness was in store somewhere. When and how were the questions? I had started working at the house on Sundays now, so I did not get the chance to go to church like I used to.

I had been invited to the annual Christmas party hosted by the ministry. It would be at the Ritz Carlton hotel in Dana Point. This was a really big deal for everyone who worked in the ministry. They had the chance to shoot the breeze with Pastor Benny and hear what he had to say about them. I had to find something nice to wear. It had been a while since I had the chance to get all dolled up. With my tight budget, I went out to Ross, a discount department store, and got a beautiful designer dress with the perfect pair of chocolate colored pumps. I pulled up to the Ritz in my little cherry red Chevy and got valet parking. With my red and chocolate dress on I thought I was cute. Inside there was food everywhere. This was exclusively for all of the employees in the California location. I heard that Pastor Benny also had a yearly Christmas celebration in Texas for the employees there.

Everyone was seated at different tables. Pastor Benny was at front and center stage with the mic in his hand, and he personally called everyone up to the mic with him and thanked them for the job that they did. I heard some of the employees say that they hoped he got their names right this year. Most of them worked in the studio location and they worked a lot behind the scenes. They were just happy to be in a more intimate setting with him other than his healing school or at his show taping for "This is Your Day."

Finally it was my turn; I was surprised that I would even be acknowledged. I had only been there since the summer. He called me up by name and he spoke of me being a hardworking single mother and even sort of remembered my son's name. He actually had me up there for a while, stating how great of a job I was doing and giving me praises. He also told me to meet with another pastor in attendance by the name of Ralph Wilkerson immediately after the event for a part time job opportunity. I was floored at the promise of another job, because maybe this was the promotion that I was hoping for financially. I was gracious for his kind words about me and the promise of more work before all the other employees. Things looked great!

I tried to get to this other pastor after the event, but Jessica told me to wait. I wanted to be obedient to what Pastor Benny had told me though; he said that I was to go up immediately after the event. I spoke with a few coworkers a little while trying to wait around, but finally, I realized that there was no way I was going to be able to talk to Pastor Wilkerson that night. Security was surrounding Pastor Benny and him, and I wanted to do as Jessica said as well, so I proceeded to say my goodbyes. I was a little disappointed about being kept from talking to Pastor Wilkerson, but I was happy with how the evening turned out.

I was saying good evening to everyone when Jessica ran over and told me to grab some food. I declined, but she insisted that I take some of the spread. I was standing there thinking, *OK, we are in the Ritz Carlton, I have on heels, and you want me to go before all of these people and snatch food from up under them?* It was laid out buffet style, so I was supposed to take this food for me and my son? I thought *not*. And again I said "No thanks," and got out of there!

Shortly after that event, one day at the house, I asked Pastor Benny after he had spoken to me, if I could ask him a question. He said sure, and I asked him about the Wilkerson job. He said he would personally call him for me, putting his hand on his head, as if he had forgot, he got up out of his chair and headed towards his office. I showed him that I appreciated his time and was excited once again about the opportunity. I had never asked Pastor Benny about any of his promises before, but I didn't want this chance to slip by.

I didn't know much about this other pastor, just that he was older and he seemed to be nice. Well, time went on and I never heard anything back from Pastor Benny about it. I just charged it to "the game." I knew that he was a man that wore many hats and he had a lot of things to do, places to be, people to see and people to save.

I thought that I would give things time to work out, but I still didn't think he had lied to me in front of those people. Maybe he just wanted to look good in front of the people, and Jessica knew it.

I did begin to notice that every time he needed something done, immediately, he would tell me that he was going to bless me financially. I naturally started to get an expectation in my heart because I wanted to take him as a man of his word, so I just continued to do my job with faith in my heart. I just was in anticipation that someday I would be blessed far beyond what I could envision by Pastor Benny. I began to have a true heart and agape love for him and his family. To me it was like getting to know a long lost relative. People are human and have their ways. I tried to understand things that were happening. I understood that people could still be anointed to do things for the Lord, yet have character flaws. *Perhaps one of his flaws was lying*, I thought.

I began to learn he was like the Michael Jackson of the televangelism world — on the streets and at home. For example, one of the things that Pastor Benny loved to do was go shopping, no matter if it was a clothing store, or a grocery store. He just liked to be out and about, doing a lot of it, in his free time. I heard that they would shut some of the local stores down so that he could walk around and shop without being bothered by fans. Shopping in Beverly Hills was his favorite local destination. Yet I had unpacked many fine pairs of leather shoes from other countries such as Italy.

When he was being driven around by his "posse" (his security) in his Mercedes, the black Suburban's and Cadillac Escalade vehicles would follow him. Even when he would drive his own vehicle (he only drove the Mercedes), the Cadillac Escalade and black Suburban vehicles would follow him.

The situation was the same in the home. There was an intercom system all over the house and security guards were everywhere, parked outside the house, throughout the house, and of course always "all around your Majesty." He also had an elaborate in-house surveillance system, including video cameras in his restroom. I often wondered if the camera was focused on him as he read the *Robb Report* magazine that was usually placed on the back of his personal commode! The *Robb Report* was a luxury magazine about exclusive vacation destinations and properties, luxury vehicles, jewelry, money reports, and other resources for the rich and famous. If he wanted to know anything all he had to do was press a button. I did not have a clue that it was this deep.

Sometimes I would feel defenseless when I would take the dog outside the home or when I was out sweeping the front sidewalk. People would drive by the house really slowly and some would ask, "Does Pastor Benny the healer live here?" I would do as I was trained and said, "No English." I didn't want to say that but, what else was I supposed to do? I didn't know these spectators! I didn't want anyone to follow me and think I had some of his "power" either. I had enough of that going on at the church.

It seemed like the majority of the people I seen that believed in him, were worshipping this man, not Jesus. People would always say that since I worked in his home a special anointing was on me, and that I had been hand selected. Pastors and "prophetesses" said that I was carrying Pastor Benny's spiritual mantel. I did not magnify on their comments. Because if they had only known what were really going on inside that house: they would have been shocked at the downright madness and dysfunction.

Once I began to realize the magnitude of the Benny Hinn worship, I felt even more mixed up. This man has influence over millions and millions of people in almost every country. People believe in this man and they give him a lot of their money. Some walked for miles in countries like Africa just to touch the hem of his garment. Television followers sent money to the ministry from TV; they give money at crusades, WHCC and the Healing School. I was always bringing the family personal gifts from the front gate from other pastors and owners of Christian television networks. It was definitely the rich blessing the rich. How could he have this "king" status when he couldn't even control his own home front? His children were hurting and his wife was suffering. I was literally losing myself in this chaos as well.

I was constantly exposed to sexually degrading apparel and objects, arguing, and constant drama in the home. One time I had to clean up after a huge Halloween bash at the parsonage. There were all sorts of things there that the ministry taught us was evil, at least in the spiritual realm. There were decorations up with spiders and spider webs, snakes, ghost, witches etc. Time and time again, I wondered how Pastor Benny could give his child money to have a Halloween party and he always spoke about demonic spirits? How could his wife tell me that she sometimes wished that she was a single mother like me? How could he allow unqualified people to run a church under his name? A church that he never visit? I began to see the hypocrisy. I could have dealt with all of this in the regular world! I was losing my belief that Benny Hinn was a real man of God.

I guess that the man started noticing that I didn't have the same spark in my walk. My spirit became so heavy and grieved that every time I walked in the parsonage my stomach began to hurt. I actually felt sick. It began to be hard for me to watch this man on TV and then see him in person; it was like he was living a double life. All of the things this man preached about and acted sincere about to his TV audience was not being practiced in his own home. One time I saw on television where people were to send in prayer requests and he was supposed to bring them to his home and pray for them. I thought, *my God. Please help.* It was scary to think that folks out there in TV land were this naïve. What was even more frightening was that I, too, had been that naïve.

I never felt any joy in the home. He was gone a lot, but either way there was no harmony. He would yell through the home, and his wife would argue with him and the children. I would hear her tell him how she didn't need him. When I would see him, before he left out of the door to travel out of the country or go out of town, you would see him standing there as if he was waiting on a hug or a blessing from his wife. I never have seen her give him that.

When he ate, he would sit in his special chair with a little table in front of him and watch TV by himself. His "everything guy" was around to make sure he didn't want anything. I thought, "what a lonely life" … I had never even seen him and his family sit around a table to eat dinner together. In fact, Christmas was the only time I had seen them all in the same room together.

One day, I was doing my job at the home and he just walked up to me with a weird look on his face, pointed his finger at me and said, "I am watching you" and walked off. His tone was that of a gangster. I thought *wow, he sounded just like the Godfather!* I felt uncomfortable and thought, Should I walk on more pins and needles now? What exactly did he mean?

I was still pondering this a few days later when I was down in the laundry room alone. Security came down to tell me to gather all of my things. I was baffled, to say the least. I took my son's picture that I had on the counter and grabbed my bag and little radio and followed him outside the front door and across the street to my car. I put everything in my car trunk and had my car keys in hand. As I was about to get into my car and leave, I asked what I had done wrong with tears in my eyes. The guard told me that Mrs. Hinn just didn't want any other woman playing music in her house. I explained that I had gotten permission, but he was adamant. Mrs. Hinn didn't want any music or pictures displayed inside her home. Dumbfounded, I said "OK, no problem," and he said that was all, that I could go back in, which I did feeling extremely awkward.

Once I got back in the laundry room, I thought *wow, are you serious?* Here I am cooped up in this tiny room most days for hours, and sometimes the only thing that made me happy was being able to look at my son's picture. Forget about the radio, but my son's picture!

Mrs. Hinn had come down into the laundry room numerous times to have so many conversations with me that I thought we were on the verge of becoming real friends. Despite her odd behavior and inconsistencies, her wacky 18-21 day fasts, her intense up and down mood swings, and how she told me she had to take sleeping pills just to go to sleep, I thought she liked me. I started to understand her more as we talked and I tried to be there for her, but then she would snap and be mean to me and I would be in tears. It was so bad at times that other seasoned staff had to take me out of the home for a break.

One day Mrs. Hinn invited me to attend the church of her friend Michelle Corral, as her special guest. The woman called me up to the altar at a church service and Mrs. Hinn came up with me. Her friend prophesied to me, telling Mrs. Hinn that the Lord had placed me in the home as a hand maiden. I was thinking, does she really need more confirmation about me, beside the dog liking me?

Regarding the music, we had had many exchanges about the singers I'd play, such as Donnie McClurkin, who mentions the Hinns' names on the back of his CD. I showed her and she claimed they loved him (he often sang at Pastor Benny's Miracle Crusades). One time she was playing a CD by CeCe Winans, who I absolutely love and when I heard her song called "We Thirst For You," it completely pulled on the strings of my heart for BHM and their home front.

Everything was starting to take a toll on me and I was increasingly getting tired and drained, physically, emotionally, and spiritually. Most times I felt like nothing more than a slave. Sometimes I would sit on the step of the lower level during a break and put my head in my hands and cry and wonder, *Lord, why am I here?* Sometimes I would take a break and go into the bathroom to just cry. I had become very confused and unhappy there. I prayed to get out of the house. I even wondered if I was being watched by Pastor Benny, as he had mentioned. Was he watching my every move?

All of a sudden, about 50 of us from Benny Hinn Ministries were laid off without any explanation. I was like, *Wow Lord! You answered my prayer!* But then I felt completely lost. My emotions were high, so of course I cried. Also there was no severance pay. BHM told me to sign something they were going to send me and I could get 400 bucks. The next day, they sent me a mini gag order via Federal Express. I tried to file for unemployment, only to find out that when you work in the ministry, you can't get unemployment, because it is a nonprofit organization.

Then it all hit me: *hey what about the other pastor he told you you would be working for? What about how he said he was going to bless you financially? What about your relationships with coworkers, church members, your pastor and his daughter? What about me and my son? What do we do now?*

I bawled and was very mixed up. Then all of a sudden, I felt a peace come over me. I knew that it was God. I got a few calls from others that worked in the ministry who were laid off, but I knew that they were only being nosy. I let them know with a weird joy that yes, I was laid off as well. They were distraught and didn't know what they were going to do with their lives, since they had given everything to the ministry. Some were from other places and were considering going back home.

They looked at me as the anointed one, so I prayed with them over the phone and that was that. Meanwhile, members of the church had found out about me being laid off as some worked in the ministry as well. Because I had been in attendance at the church on Sundays again, word quickly got around. They would say, "How could they lay you off? Aren't you are a single mom? But God chose you to be in that house!" I shrugged, unknowing. I wasn't sure of anything anymore.

A week or so had passed when I got a call from the BHM, stating they needed me back at the house. *Huh? Seriously?* I immediately accepted. I accepted because prophetic words had been spoken over me at my former church FCC and WHCC. FCC was in contact with me from time to time and Pastor Munsey would come tape shows for "This is Your Day" with Pastor Benny. I didn't want to say to them that I didn't go back. Both they and I were looking forward to great things happening.

Some of my former church members at FCC even wanted me to talk to Pastor Benny personally about their situations, yet I told them that it was not that easy. So I went back to the parsonage thinking that it must have been the Lord working on their hearts concerning me.

Later I heard that they do this lay off thing fairly often for the books. Georgia, at the headquarters, told me that since I was in the parsonage when I went back that I was not employed under Benny Hinn ministries anymore. Instead, my job would be based on a contract between Pastor Benny and me directly. I thought this was a good move. *Wow! A contract between Pastor Benny and me personally? Thank you Lord, my dreams of getting off of government systems are finally here.* I begin to get extremely excited. *Wow, I must be about to get paid very well.*

5

GETTING PAID?

Well, I got my job back. I guess that I was glad that they wanted me to come back. I figured that this was a new beginning, and I still enjoyed the drive in the mornings. I was feeling that the promises from Pastor Benny would finally be fulfilled: I was back in a position to be blessed. I looked at it as a turning point and that maybe I was just not grateful enough before. Since I had been so critical in my thoughts, I felt that maybe God wanted to teach me a lesson. After all another thing that was taught to us was keeping our thoughts pure.

Once I got back to work I resumed my normal duties. I didn't have as many hours as before and I didn't know what my pay rate would be, but I assumed it would surely be more than before. I couldn't wait for the opportunity to sit down with Pastor Benny and discuss business, so I continued working in the feeling of being chosen. I definitely felt that God had called me to be there and it was not by coincidence that I was back.

I got back and Mrs. Hinn was as friendly as ever. She and I would talk and it was better than before. She would tell me about her new calling and how it was now her turn to be in the spotlight. That it was far too long that she had been in the shadows of Pastor Benny. She would tell me about how much heartache her daughter, my pastor's wife, had caused her. She sounded very mad and resentful towards Jessica for some reason.

She told me about how everyone was jealous of her being Pastor Benny's wife. She told me how even her girlfriends envied her lifestyle, and how she couldn't trust anyone. She always told me how she hated living in California and that it was not her idea to move there. She told me that it was good that I was a single parent and sometimes she wished she was single again. After these laments, we talked and prayed and I thought I had begun to understand her further. After all, I was there and if she was lonesome and needed someone to vent to, I was willing to try to learn to be a more understanding listener. I believed that I was being prepped for the ministry. Besides, nuts come in all sizes, so I had to study how to deal with the big ones and the little ones.

Finally, I got approval for a day off on my son's 7th birthday in January of 2006! I had asked for the day weeks in advance and was told that everything would be covered. I had worked holidays and his birthday was a couple of weeks after Christmas. I had never taken off before. Sometimes I would work over 10 days straight without a break. I needed to spend some time with my son. I mean, you only get one 7th birthday and I was the only parent that's ever been involved in his life. So I took off.

With the food stamps I received, I was able to go get my son a birthday cake, drinks and snacks. It was going to be all about him that day. We gave him a party at WHCC with most of his little friends from the church. He had so much fun and it felt great to see him happy.

After that, I had a little money I had saved to take him out to Chuck E. Cheese for pizza later that evening with another single mother who attended the church. She was homeless and her son and my son became good friends. We would go out to eat sometimes or they would come over to my place, so we had fun celebrating my son's birthday that evening. Little did I know I would be confronted by Mrs. Hinn the moment I got back to work!

When I got back to work Mrs. Hinn confronted me in the hallway right next to the laundry room, at the top of her voice and in my face. She yelled, "Why weren't you here?" Staggered, I stated to her that it was my son's birthday and told her that I had received approval to be off, but before I could get anything else out she yelled, "This is Benny Hinn Ministries! I don't think you understand who we are; we are on the forefront of ministry here! I don't know what you did over at Pastor Munsey's but we are Benny Hinn Ministries and we don't take days off!" She huffed and puffed and yelled with rage, "I can't even remember the last time my husband was here on my birthday or any of the children's, so that is not an excuse!"

I apologized profusely, more than a little bewildered, and she said, "Well, I know that you are not full time now, so what are you going to do? Are you looking for other work? Because I know that you can't make it here in Orange County off of just this." I was completely speechless. She had let me know that she was aware of what I was getting paid before and it gave me a clue that I shouldn't expect much more. But she went on, "I am beginning to feel like it is too ritzy for me here; I wish that I was back in Florida! I hate it here!" She took a breath. "So what are you going to do? Can you go back to Chicago to Pastor Steve's ministry? Maybe you can work for them?" I stated that I was not moving back to Chicago. She told me that, "I know that you feel like God has you here, but this job alone is not going to be enough." I was in tears once again when she walked away.

Sue was around and she suggested that we take a break, and we went to Starbucks where she called her husband to join us. I was very upset. That is when I made them aware that I had not met with Pastor Benny or anyone concerning my pay.

I had been back in the house for weeks now and I had not yet known anything about being paid. I would go in on the weekends a lot and I would have to have a babysitter for my son. Also, I had no savings. I was living paycheck to paycheck. The paychecks were just enough to give money to the church, pay bills and get gas. I was the working poor as it was and I hadn't got a check. I sure couldn't buy gas with food stamps. I was starting to get nervous and so I had to ask Sue again about my pay. She told me that she was going to check with her husband to see what she could find out. He was like a liaison between Pastor Benny and I. I waited and waited and asked her a few days later, but they hadn't heard anything. She and her husband knew that I was running on empty, so they gave me a little cash. I was very grateful for their donation, but I was very bothered.

I briefed the couple that watched my son on Christmas on the pay situation. To my surprise they told me of how the Hinns feel that just being in their presence was your pay and the fact that you get to serve them is your compensation. I was not trying to hear of this sick, twisted type of pay. I needed some real answers. They suggested that I ask Pastor Benny for the money directly. They told me that if I waited for anyone else that this could take forever. They also informed me that if I did ask him about money that he might get mad, but that I should be able to get something out of him as if he was hard up.

Even though I worked in his home, it was like he was untouchable, and everyone was a yes man. No one wanted to speak up for anything or anybody. There was no one that I could ask for help, at least no one that I knew. Everyone that I knew in the ministry was broke, busted, and disgusted! Things were starting to get bad quick and I needed money for gas just to get to work. The soles of my son's shoes were worn and I needed to buy him a new pair. I was working and not getting paid for my labor. I had to do something quick ….

6

EXCUSE ME SIR?

Well, what can I say, here I was working for one of the most famous and wealthiest televangelists in the world, and I was parked in the 76 gas station praying for enough nerve to ask a stranger for a few bucks for gas to get to work. I had left home about an hour ahead of my usual time this particular day, with just enough gas to get to the service station. I knew that I had to get to work because I could not afford to lose my position, especially with the shenanigans Mrs. Hinn was pulling. I sat in the car for a bit, thinking that perhaps someone would think something was wrong with me and ask, but no one ever did. *Well, here I go.* A woman around my age walked into the station and she looked like she wouldn't be alarmed if I approached her.

"Uhhh, excuse me ma'am?"

"Yes?"

"I'm stranded; can I please have a couple of dollars for gas, please?" She reached in her purse and gave it to me. "Thank you so much, and may God bless you."

Whew, that was so embarrassing. But I had three dollars for gas to get to work, and I was rolling. Feeling like a loser and desperate, I started to actually toy with the idea of approaching the "man himself," as nerve-wracking as it was. He knew that I was a single parent, and maybe he would even remember the promises of money and the other job opportunity he told me about. But I had my doubts. *Naah, I can't possibly go to him, he is much too busy and important for me.* I shook my head.

I made it on into work. Pulling up to the parsonage that day was especially hard. My son needed a new pair of shoes and I was irritated and disturbed to not have gotten paid. I was even running low on basic necessities around my place. I just didn't know how much longer this could go on. To me, it was not just about the money, but the principle of the situation.

I was fluffing sofa pillows in the living area when along came Mrs. Hinn. She started just talking about how the guy that was serving as Pastor Benny's armor bearer was not worthy to be in his position, that he was too young and too inexperienced to be his armor bearer and how she was about to make it known that she did not like him! She said that she wanted to get rid of him. I was really disappointed in her judgment and lofty reasoning. It seems as though the young man was doing a great job to me.

That is why they wanted young unmarried folks in the house, unless you were a couple like Sue and her husband. I had heard that if I got married it may be a problem for me. I thought, *this woman does not have a clue of what it feel like to serve any of you Hinn's.* At this point I thought to myself that she had no discernment, no respect for herself, her husband, her children, me, or anyone else! This woman was so selfish! She didn't have an inkling of what it was like to be a servant. If only she could get a hint that day that I could care less about her meaningless chatter. If she could see the look on my face, she would get a huge clue that something was awfully wrong with me. She was supposed to be so spiritual and prophetic. *Can you tell me when I will get paid?* I thought. *Can you tell me if I will make it home on the fumes that are in my tank? Can you tell me that lady?*

I sat there and listened to her, but I knew that I could not tell her about the money situation. I was sitting there listening to her complain about her life, while she had brochures of new homes, cars and a $500 box of chocolates sitting on the counter from Beverly Hills. Do you think a sister could have asked her to borrow a couple of bucks? She did not care about anything but what she wanted. She was blind.

I continued my duties after her whining session. When I got off, I knew that I would not have enough gas to make it home. I went to a gas station there in Dana Point and asked a couple of people for help but they declined. I left because I did not want to get into trouble. The last thing I needed was to be bust out and plastered in the town paper for panhandling while working for Benny Hinn Ministries or worse, lose my job. So I went to the Gelson's that I always went to to shop for the house. They had a gas station nearby and there I went again. "Excuse me sir? Can you please help me so that I can have gas to get back home?" Kindly, he did. I prayed that none of their security would see me panhandling up there as it was only a few minutes down the street.

I made it home and picked up my son from my neighbors upstairs who were doctors. They were from Persia and they just loved my son. They would watch him for me because they knew that I was on call for the Hinn's as well. They would even take him into their office on a Saturday if they had to. I remember one time they came back home and they were so excited to tell me about an agency that handled child actors and models. While they were out in Orange County this agency had seen my son and they were very interested, so I started the process to get my son involved. They were great people, always inviting us up for delicious dinners, and they were already doing so much to help me by watching my son. I would never want to ask them for money.

When it was time for me to go to work again, I had to do this panhandling all over again and it got to be unbearably degrading. I remember one day I panhandled for money to get to work, and as soon as I walked in the door Mrs. Hinn told me that I could go home. She had done this quite a few times, but it was especially frustrating this day. Hmm ... didn't the prophetess know what I had to go through to get here today? Couldn't she have just called me? I drove home on fumes, broke, busted and disgusted! I went forward with my day and decided that I was going to spend this Saturday with my son, having fun, regardless of the bad start. I went into the condo and got some snacks, went and grabbed him from upstairs and we walked to the park. We swung on the swings, played catch, and had a good time. He was smiling and happy. I looked down at his tattered shoes while we were at the park and reality hit again, but I was not going to let it rain on our parade.

When we got home and he went to sleep, he looked so adorable. I cried a river of tears because all I ever wanted to do was give him the world, and here I was, not knowing what kind of mess I had gotten us into once again. I felt manipulated and deceived. When people are facing challenges in life and have already been dealt a heck of a hand, nothing else makes you angrier than being penniless! I knew that I could not carry on like this. It had gotten to the point where I was calling my friend Alesha just to vent all the time. She was a single parent of three and she was very much involved at FCC. She is one of the best friends a person could ever have. Sometimes I don't know what I would have done without her.

I was so out of it sometimes. I believe that I was so drawn in and sold out for the ministry that I had lost myself. I felt abused on all sorts of levels and it hurt, very badly. Could it have been that I was brainwashed, bamboozled, scammed, something? Between Pastor Benny Hinn's swindling and Mrs. Hinn's new religious endeavors, I was disillusioned. There was no way that I could ever believe that these people would have put me in an awful situation out here like this.

I had heard from insiders about how the Hinns felt that your pay was "being allowed" to serve them. They thought that you should survive on the privilege, and they had me to serve them in the most degrading, lowliest ways possible. They did not discriminate, they wanted everyone to serve them hand and foot. For example, Pastor Benny's hairstylist came to the parsonage personally to do his signature hairdo. He wanted everything done by hand. I had to even wash Mrs. Hinn's undergarments by hand, when they could have easily taken more things to the cleaners. They were obsessed with this servitude thing. There was even talk of a personal chef from New York coming to work in the parsonage,

I was seeing and talking to people who had been in the ministry for years working for peanuts. There were people that had relocated from other states and countries just to serve in the ministry and a lot of them were not paid a dime. The only people receiving decent pay that I knew of were his immediate family: his wife, his son-in-law Michael (who was my pastor), and his daughter Jessica. All them were on the payroll and had plush offices, but what did they do exactly?

I had heard and seen enough and all I wanted to know at this point was "Can I get my money?" My friend Alesha suggested that I go directly to the man. I didn't know how that would turn out, but I knew that I could not continue to work for these people for free.

7

FIRED

After a pep talk from my friend Alesha I was convinced I needed to go directly to the man. I knew that he had been out of town but he had come back early. Alesha suggested I go in immediately to see about my money, spoken like a true Illinois lady, yet I was thinking that I should give him some time to rest. I kept making excuses to myself. I just waited a little longer, and a little longer. On my next day off, I knew that Benny Hinn was at home. I looked down at my son's shoes and thought about how I did not want to panhandle anymore, so I got up enough courage to go and ask Pastor Benny about my pay. I had a little gas left in my tank from panhandling to go on out to Dana Point, so I got in the car and prayed that everything would work out.

I did not want to be out of line in any way, shape or form. I was praying that I would be received and understood with open arms, and I was hoping that he would just write me a check out and everything would be smooth. Anything would have helped.

I went through the gate with my pass and parked my car where I normally park, which was across the street from the parsonage. I nervously got out of my car and walked up to the door. This door never looked so big to me. It was very tall and wide. In fact, I always went through the garage, and the only time I would be by the front door was when I was cleaning spider webs off of it. *Ok, deep breaths ....* I know that my face was red because I turn red from everything, laughing, crying, being mad, blushing. OK, you get the picture.

I rang the doorbell and Sue opened the door, surprised to see me. Pastor Benny was coming out of his office that was right by the front door and said, "Hi Cheryl, come in."

In front of Sue I said, "Pastor I don't want to be out of line but do you have a moment?" He said he did, and I thought that he would invite me into his office but we stood right there in the entryway. I proceeded to tell him how I knew he was very busy and that I felt embarrassed bringing this to him, but I had not been paid in almost a month. He immediately said I should call Georgia at Benny Hinn Ministries. I told him that I called her, but she said that I was not paid under the ministry anymore.

He looked like he could care less. In his silence, I explained to him how I was told that I was employed directly by him rather than through the ministry. He gave me the nastiest look and seemed very angry. Nervously, I told him that I was sorry and that I would have never brought this to him, and I was waiting for a liaison to contact him on my behalf, but it had come to the point where I literally had nothing. I told him it had been very difficult for my son and me.

He threw his hands up and with a hateful look on his face, he yelled, "I don't handle this!" He paused then, as if I were going to say something. I didn't know what else to say so I said again, "I am sorry", but he became irate with me even more! He kept yelling, "I don't handle this! I don't handle this! I don't do this!" One of his security team came downstairs looking sympathetic towards me.

With shock and embarrassment on my face, I felt myself going numb. He looked at me in a way that I will never forget, like *how dare you approach me you dog!* (That is what I got in my spirit, but it could have been worse). I was frozen. I could not move! I cannot even remember the other things that were coming out of his mouth, because at this point his words and body movements were in slow motion.

The more he ranted the less human I felt. All I can remember after that is him yelling at me with the most evil tone in his voice, saying, "Go to the studio! Go to the studio!" Meanwhile, he was opening the door and backing me out of the house. I knew then that that would be my last time there. As I stepped across the threshold of the door, he slammed the door so hard behind me that I thought that it would break!

There I stood on the front porch trembling, crying, and perplexed. I was terrified and heartbroken. I knew that it was over. I felt a pain in my head and in my stomach. I couldn't move or breathe; it felt as though I was having an out-of-body experience, watching myself go through this scenario. I cried uncontrollably as I began to walk slowly down the stairs, feeling dizzy and like I would faint. I walked out the front gate and across the street to my car dazed. I turned around and looked at the house one more time, then sat there in my car a few minutes to get myself together to try to make it to the studio.

With no money in my pocket, I scrounged around in my car looking for any change that might have fallen on the floor. As tears rolled down my face, I gathered about 85 cents total and I hoped that I had enough gas to get from Dana Point to the studio in Aliso Viejo, I started my car and the gas light was on. I rolled down the street and out the front gates of the community waving goodbye to the guard at the front gate.

I began to weep again as I drove past Salt Creek Beach, which was where I would pass every day on my way to work. My tears were like a thunderstorm rain, hitting your windshield so hard you can't see. Even the windshield wipers and defogger could not clear up this vision. I felt like my vision was now totally blurred in every area of my life. I was struggling to get to the light, and when I did, it burned me. I drove to the studio blinded by my tears and with fumes in my gas tank! Instead of "This is Your Day," this wasn't my day at all! I finally made it to the studio.

When I got inside the studio, security was waiting for me. They looked at me as if I had taken something. They walked me into a room and told me I was fired. They told me I was not permitted to go to the parsonage nor the studio, not even for a show taping for "This is Your Day." They asked me for my badges, and before I could try to tell them anything, they stopped me and asked me, "Do you know who he is?" They told me that there was a protocol, just like there is for a president or a king, that I should have known that I could not just pop up at the parsonage.

They told me to just go on, and live my life and that "I better not ever go against Benny Hinn Ministries or that my family and I will be cursed." They told me that people who had left from BHM go on and do great things for the Lord, but that there are also ones that have died once they have gone against BHM. They assured me that God will still use me if I did not go against the ministry. They reminded me that they had a quick turnover; especially at the parsonage, and that I had longevity there compared to others. They said that I was to wait for Georgia from the headquarters to contact me about getting paid...

By then I was crying uncontrollably. "Could I just get a moment?" I asked them. I went to the restroom to wipe my pitiful face, and then they escorted me out of the building and wished me luck. Just like that it was over.

I was embarrassed, because there was other staff around staring at me as I walked out the building. I got into my car and immediately got out of there, feeling like I was still having an out of body experience. I knew that I had tried, God knows I tried, but for some reason I always got thrown away. I felt like a hopeless piece of nothing, like I didn't deserve to even have been in the position that I was in in the first place.

I drove to the nearest gas station to put my 85 cents in my tank because my gas light was on. I still had no money. I had to ask someone to help me again with the gas. I was crying when I did and they helped me out. *I have nothing now,* I thought. *Maybe I should have just held on a little longer. Maybe I shouldn't have listened to my coworkers or Alesha.* I was angry at myself a long while for listening to Alesha, even though she was the only true friend I had. I just could not believe it all ended this way. *I came here with nothing and now I had tripled nothing. What about all of the prophecies and promises? What do I do now? Jessica had gotten me the job, would she be angry with me? Was her husband, my pastor, going to be angry? Would I continue to go to the church? He did give me one tip before?* I was so devastated.

Within the next few days I got a call from Georgia at the headquarters and she told me to give her my hours. I told her my hours and she told me what the amount of pay would be at the rate of 10 dollars per hour. I told her no, that I had worked on holidays and weekends, and that I should be paid at a higher rate. I had my contract drawn up and I told her my rate, which was the going rate in the area. She said that I was trying to price gouge them and get over on the ministry. Her voice was dripping with nastiness. But I was adamant that these were the going rates in Orange County for half of what I did. I also wanted double time for my holiday and weekend hours. I would not settle for less, and after going back and forth with Georgia, I finally got paid what I requested several days later and that was the end of that.

Still needing support, my son and I went to church, where I would try to reach out to Pastor Michael but he would ignore me after church. Sometimes I would be crying while standing in line to talk to him, and he would leave with his security. I felt very much rejected, so I set up an appointment with him for spiritual guidance with his associate Pastor Scott Wead. Scott told me that it will be okay. He told me that he remembered when Pastor Benny had wanted some blueberries when they were in New York and they had to run all over town to find him the perfect blueberries in the freezing cold, and when we finally came back to the hotel with them he was mad because it took so long. "So that is just how he is," he said. "I have cried plenty of times when he has hurt my feelings, and that is just how ministry is. You must go through the fire to come out as pure gold."

I finally got to speak to Pastor Michael and he along with Pastor Scott suggested that I let this lady in the church named

Marcia move in with me. I told Pastor Michael what he already knew, which was that I was on government housing and that I could not have anyone live with me on a long term basis. Plus, this woman was legally blind and partially deaf. I did not know if I could handle her. Pastor Michael told me that he was happy that his tax dollars went to help people like me. I thought *'People like me!' OK, wow!* That is when it really sank in that I came there with nothing, and I had lost more than I had when I came there to serve people like *them*. People who like to keep their foot on your neck.

He proceeded to tell me that he would give me 200 dollars for the first month to let this woman Marcia from the church stay with me and my son. 200 dollars to take care of this lady, are you serious? I was thinking, *Is that all you think of me? Was this his way of giving me a job?* But I was weak and I felt sorry for this woman's situation, so Pastors Michael and Scott arranged to have all of her things moved into my place. I assumed we all could figure something out for her long-term later.

This woman was being evicted from her apartment. She was a senior-citizen and I just couldn't leave her in the streets. She had also been a faithful woman to WHCC in her sacrificial giving. She was one of the ones I would give a ride to back to her apartment, or wait with her at the bus stop. I was sure that if I was not so messed up over my just getting fired, I would be able to help her better. What I quickly found out was that once Michael and Scott got her inside my home they were finished with the situation and done dealing with her, so I was their dumping ground yet again. I mean, they literally moved this lady and all of her things into my home and when she started running me into the ground, they Would not even help me get her out of my place and into a shelter.

In addition to the nature at hand, I discovered more than I originally knew: the dear woman had several other major health problems. She used to choke on things, have breathing issues, and severe mood swings. It was too much to bear, and finally some people she knew came to move her out. I was very disappointed at how Pastor Michael and Scott cared nothing about my personal living space. I received no money from them for her, nor did I want any money. Pastor Scott told me that the reason for them treating her that way was because it was in the Bible: that if she did not listen to them she should be treated like a tax collector. Now that was the most ignorant thing I had ever heard from a "pastor." I was not even about to go there on the widow and orphan scriptures. So my question was, if they felt like that, then why would they want to put her on me and my son when I already had so much to deal with? I guess they wanted to put their version of waste in the same can.

*From Alesha   Page 1 of 1

Subject: *From Alesha
  Date: Mon, Mar 6, 2006 10:43 am

Dear Cheryl,

I really hope you are feeling better...I realize this morning was really difficult for you especially after everything you and _____ have been thru this past weekend. I just want to reassure you that everything I said to Marcia was necessary but I in no way was disrespectful or rude to her over the phone. As soon as I said today needs to be her last day there, she starting going off and accused me of not being a Christian. It really does not bother me because after hearing her voice, in my spirit I realize this woman is not stable and she desperately needs Jesus. I pray that God will give her direction and guidance but the fact that she has income of disability, although it's probably not much money Marcia needs to depend on God because He truly is our source of everything. Again I want to emphasize that she needs to cry and most importantly cry out to God because this woman is playing on your sympathy Cheryl. She is wrong and has not been a respectful guest to you during the short time she has been in your house. Please do not allow the enemy to use this woman any longer. I hope when I talk to you later Marcia will be gone. Remember since your name is on the lease you can always call the police and they will escort her to a shelter and you can make arrangements for her other things to be sent to her. Cheryl, Marcia being in your home is hindering what God wants to do for you. Go to God yourself and He will show you. Love you girl! Get some rest and I will talk to you later okay.

Alesha

Letter from Alesha to me about Marcia

Later, I went to church and met with Pastor Michael. He strongly recommended that I move back home, or to Texas. I didn't know why he suggested that I move anywhere, but I was just glad that he was talking to me again. I didn't know much about Texas and he explained it to me. He told me that my son and I would fit in perfectly there. He said that I was still a part of the ministry, and to let him know what I was going to do. I asked if he would help with the move if that was where I decided to go, and he told me that he would think about it.

When I visited church he would overlook me as much as he could. After that, I started to feel bad and hurt all over again, so I just disappeared from the church. I figured if no one called, no one cared. Plus, I needed to really understand everything that had transpired. A few weeks went by. I didn't hear from anyone. The silence spoke volumes.

8

BREAKDOWN

During the time I was away from the church, I was so out of it. I felt down, depressed, shaky and even suicidal. I was in survival mode and realized that this Benny Hinn business was too much for me to grasp. How could he fire a single mother for letting him know that she wasn't getting paid? I, for the life of me, could not understand this. He talked one thing and preached another. *He is a phony, a fraud, a liar, and he disrespected me,* I thought.

After I stopped going to church, I was unable to function. As soon as my son went to school, I would sleep all day. He was in the first grade, and I had him in an afterschool program at the school. I dreaded walking up the street to pick him up. I just did not want to get out of bed. I did, however, have a friend named Stacey from the church whose son was friends with my son. I called her to tell her of what happened, and she came over to have us follow her to another church. We went inside and a pastor prayed for me. I tried to feel better.

We were supposed to try to go to a prayer meeting somewhere else that evening, but as I drove on the way there I started having sharp pains coming and going through my head, so I went to the nearest hospital in Irvine. Stacey followed me. I was crying and shaking with my son in the car. I tried to park the best I could near the emergency room entrance. My son was terrified.

I got out of the car and fell to the ground. I felt like I was going to die. I was on my knees in the parking lot of the hospital hollering, "Jesus please help me, please help me, why? I don't want to die!"

I remember at some point my friend ran to get help and my son was screaming "Mommy, mommy!" and crying with fear. I don't remember much more about the incident, but I was suffering mentally, physically, and spiritually. The E.R. wanted to check me into a psychiatric ward, but I did not have anyone long-term to care for my child, so I had to pull myself together quickly. They prescribed Xanax. I went home and was grateful my son had calmed down. I felt so badly about breaking down in front of him. That had never happened to me before.

I had always tried to be a good parent, protecting my boy from harm; I never wanted him to get abused like I had been. I always keep a close eye on him. My job was to protect him but I never knew that hurt could come in this form, with all of these complexities. I was beginning to feel like a terrible mother and that he deserved someone better than me to raise him. I was thinking about how my own mother had told me that I was a wasted ejaculation and how she wishes she would have aborted me. I thought about how from the beginning of my existence I had been rejected, abused and abandoned.

Now, here I was at the forefront of a healing ministry, getting the door slammed on me, and the so-called "man of God" looks down on me like I am a dog. I felt like I was useless. I mean, how do you get fired from cleaning toilets? How? I felt such despair. I was ashamed of just being me. All my life people had abused me sexually, physically, and emotionally, and now I was being abused spiritually by Benny Hinn and his crew. People that I felt I should be able to trust! *Who can I trust?* I thought. *Who is there left to trust?*

I was trying my best to cope with the situation, I felt I had no support system. This had been the first time in my life that I had really felt like I was a part of something real, something that

I believed in. But now, I felt very isolated. I took my Xanax and slept even more, but I had to pull it together for my son, who I knew was also suffering emotionally.

We had started working with some places in Studio City for my son to get started in the entertainment industry, but I was in no condition at that point to even discuss business. My son would be excited and ask questions because I had taken him on an audition for a McDonald's commercial, and they loved him. It was his first time and it looked very promising. I felt so guilty for not being able to handle this business for him like I was supposed to.

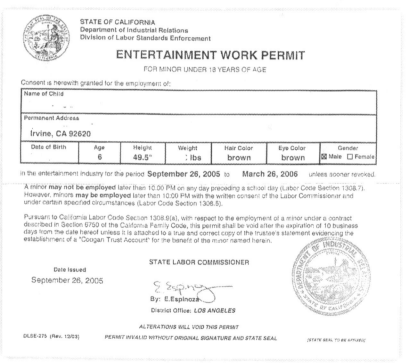

STATE OF CALIFORNIA
Department of Industrial Relations
Division of Labor Standards Enforcement

ENTERTAINMENT WORK PERMIT

FOR MINOR UNDER 18 YEARS OF AGE

Consent is herewith granted for the employment of:

Name of Child

Permanent Address

Irvine, CA 92620

Date of Birth	Age	Height	Weight	Hair Color	Eye Color	Gender
	6	49.5"	: lbs	brown	brown	☒ Male ☐ Female

in the entertainment industry for the period **September 26, 2005** to **March 26, 2006** unless sooner revoked.

A minor may not be employed later than 10:00 PM on any day preceding a school day (Labor Code Section 1308.7). However, minors **may be employed** later than 10:00 PM with the written consent of the Labor Commissioner and under certain specified circumstances (Labor Code Section 1308.5).

Pursuant to California Labor Code Section 1308.9(a), with respect to the employment of a minor under a contract described in Section 6750 of the California Family Code, this permit shall be void after the expiration of 10 business days from the date hereof unless it is attached to a true and correct copy of the trustee's statement evidencing the establishment of a "Coogan Trust Account" for the benefit of the minor named herein.

STATE LABOR COMMISSIONER

Date Issued
September 26, 2005

By: E.Espinoza

District Office: *LOS ANGELES*

ALTERATIONS WILL VOID THIS PERMIT

DLSE-275 (Rev. 12/03)   *PERMIT INVALID WITHOUT ORIGINAL SIGNATURE AND STATE SEAL*   [STATE SEAL TO BE AFFIXED]

My son's entertainment work permit

But, it was about staying sane at that point. I felt fragile, like I was a raw egg and if you dropped me, I would crack. I just know that if it was not for my son, I would have ended it once and for all.

I had started to feel empty and I had not heard anything at all from my church. I was very lonely, desperate, and confused. One day I decided to take a drive, and soon, I found myself in a Buddhist temple in town. They were so nice to me; they did not judge me, at all. And even though I decided Buddhism was not the right path for me and my son, I was very grateful to have come in contact with such loving people.

Another day, I went to the Trinity Broadcasting Network (TBN) building in Costa Mesa. They absolutely loved Pastor Benny Hinn. I spent some time there watching movies and praying in the prayer room. I needed someone to talk to and pray with, but unfortunately there was no one there for that. I then found myself at the South Coast Plaza, one of the richest malls in America. I had been there before for lunch with some BHM staff in the past and we had walked around the mall dreaming and naming and claiming things. I don't know if I was reminiscing or going down memory lane, but I knew one thing, I was getting a little low on gas. So I actually asked a few people inside and outside the mall for money. I got about 5 dollars, and I went to go buy a beverage.

On the way to the food court, a lady said hi to me. I was anxious to talk to someone, so I asked her if she could help me with gas. I guess my panhandling demons had jumped back out. She gave me a 10 dollar bill and invited me to lunch … now that was the most I had ever got panhandling! She was so nice, and she was a Christian too. It was like God had sent someone to talk to me. We said a little prayer and she even had me follow her to a place where they gave women discounts on secondhand designer clothing. Since I was back on the market for employment, she actually bought me a few items, and the day was rich and encouraging. Because of her acts of kindness, I began to get a little confidence back. I even decided that I was going to make it.

One evening, out the blue, Jessica called me and asked me why I had not been to church. I explained everything that had been happening, and she asked me what I was going to do. I told her that I did not know, and she asked what she could do to help. I told her about how Pastor Michael had spoken to me about Texas, and how he felt it would be better for us there and I pondered moving, but I needed help financially to do anything. She told me that she would pray about helping. I also told her that I was on Xanax and she told me to stop taking them, because she had been on them before and that they were very addictive.

She also told me to not let what her father did leave a sour taste in my mouth. She told me that my son and I should come back to the church. She sounded sincere, but I thought about how Pastor Michael had acted towards me the last time I was there. I thought about how he snubbed me, and how he had played the situation with Marcia, and it bothered me that he was urging me to move out of town. But, I knew that most of all I needed the Lord. I had been taught that I needed to be under a spiritual covering, and I felt that my son had grown accustomed to being at the church and that we missed it there. Jessica seemed to be very concerned about us coming back to church. It was good that she called. I still believed in the vision of the church, and I thought that I needed God more than anything and that nothing else mattered.

I needed answers, and I wanted to consider the best situation. Besides, Pastor Michael would always say, "Bring the fish in and leave it up to me and the Lord to clean them." I didn't know what the atmosphere would be like, and I wasn't sure how Pastor Michael would act, but I knew that I needed the Lord more than anything right now to live. So I decided that my son and I should head back to church.

Pastor Michael and Jessica's Happy New Year card

9

THE EXIT SIGN

With tears in my eyes I write this chapter, as it is extremely difficult to start. Where do I start? I get so emotional from the memories of all of this and the damage that it has done to me and my son's life. Still bruised, I go into this chapter, because I still cannot believe that this happened!

It was on a Wednesday Bible study night that I decided to return back to church. Typically at least eight or so of us would gather in prayer an hour before service. When my son and I got to WHCC, we were greeted by Pastor Scott Wead and a few other members. They were happy to see us and we were happy to be back at church. Even though things didn't work out at Pastor Benny's, it was my prayer that the Lord would convict him to the point where he would make things right with me.

I gave my son a hug and sat him in the sanctuary as I always did before I went into the room that we used for prayer. My son knew the routine, even though we had not been there in a while. Sometimes I would have him come in when we prayed, but this time, I knew that I was going to need a little extra something. I was searching for answers to some of the questions in my head. I didn't know what to do. Why did I now have to decide where I was going to live? And I didn't know why my life was so screwed up. I was fragile, down, and brokenhearted, and I also wanted the prayer warriors to pray with me about my son's wellbeing. I was anticipating a word from the Lord, a breakthrough, or *something* that night to thrust me forward.

I waited in that room along with another woman for the others to come. We waited and waited and after about ten minutes it was unusual for no one else to be there. Suddenly, we heard footsteps coming down the hall, and it was Lungo, Pastor Michael's security guard. I was happy to see him; I said hello and asked where everyone was. I had not been there in a while, so I wondered if something had changed. Lungo asked me to come with him. I got up and walked towards him, and then he told me to get my things. I got my things, and then he told me that I was no longer welcome there at the church.

I was in disbelief. "Excuse me?" I asked. He said that my son and I had to leave and that we were not welcome at WHCC any longer. I told him that Jessica had called me and asked us to come back to church herself. He told me that I was to leave immediately!

Walking back down the hall towards the sanctuary, I saw the assistant Pastor Scott Wead, and called out to him, but he ignored me. At that point other security were visible, and Lungo told me to get my son and leave and that I was not permitted to talk to anyone there. I got my son out of the sanctuary, Lungo still by my side. My son looked confused as he saw my tear-stained face and asked me, "Mommy what's wrong?" I told him that God had everything under control. I was still thinking that this was all a terrible mistake or misunderstanding.

I asked Lungo how he could kick a single mother and child out of the church: I pay my tithes here, I serve here, and we are members. My son has friends here! Sobbing, I asked him why. He told me that I was a security risk. I did not even know what a security risk was! He said, "Look, I know that this is wrong, but I'm just doing my job, OK? I have to do what they tell me to do, and you know how they are." We walked out of the church.

I said, "How could you get up and testify in church and call yourself a man of God doing this?" I told him that I wanted to wait to speak to Pastor Michael, and then Lungo told me to leave immediately in a stern voice. My son was clinging to me, terrified. This big tall Samoan man that we had grown to know and love at church was now acting like a stranger. He would always speak to my son or pat his head and make small talk with him. Now this?

I told him if he knew that it was wrong then he should stand up and do what is right, and he said, "After all that they have done for you?" I could see that he was under their spell, convinced that I was an ingrate.

My friend Stacey was walking toward the church as I was leaving in tears. She looked confused and asked, "Cheryl what's wrong?" I told her that they were kicking us out of the church. Other security was visible outside and Lungo told me not to make a scene as he prompted Stacey to go into the building. He continued to escort us to our car, and we got in and locked the doors.

As soon as we were inside the car, my son said, "Mom, I thought they were going to shoot us." I was so upset about my son making that statement and how everything had gone down that I drove down the hill and waited until Pastor Michael drove up. I wanted to see him face to face.

Sure enough, five minutes later he drove up and I followed him right back up that hill. I parked my car and got out and yelled, "Pastor Michael!" But he did not answer. Instead, he got on his cell phone and I asked, "Why, Pastor Michael? How could you do this to us?" He continued walking into the building, like a coward, as if he did not see my son and me. I guess at that time I had no pride or dignity left; I was so pathetic. My son even had the sense to say, "Mom, let's just go."

Security came back out and told me that if I did not leave they would have me arrested for trespassing. I was so disappointed and lost, and I felt so guilty for having my son go through another terrible ordeal. I felt so rejected and could only imagine my child feeling the same way. I thought about how Jessica had told me she would pray to see if she would help me financially, and wondered if she knew anything about this. I tried to call her after that fiasco, but her number was disconnected. I had a nagging sense she knew this was going to happen.

My son's heart was broken, because he had been looking forward to seeing his little friends that night and here we were being kicked out the church before he could ever say goodbye. But he was the stronger one; he wound up encouraging me in the midst of the drama. He gave me hugs and when I told him I loved him, he told me he loved me more. I went home that evening and every night after that I would try to always wait until my son went to sleep before I cried and pondered my dilemma. And when he was at school, I would go for a ride and cry. I wanted to put the best face on possible for him because I did not want to break his beautiful spirit anymore. I didn't understand, so how could I expect a little boy that is merely 7 years old to understand?

I cried many tears, and after all I had been through with these people, I was too numb. All I could think about was the look on my son's face when they kicked us out of the church. I thought it was a crying shame to get kicked out of a church. It was supposed to be a healing ministry.

I got the creepiest feelings at night. Sometimes, while I was driving, I would look out my rear view mirror, and what did you know, it appeared the boys were following me.

10

INTIMIDATION

There I was, a mess driving down the street, still thinking about what had transpired and what do you know, it looked like one of the ministry's black Suburban's was a few cars back. So I did a couple of turns, and I peeped through my rearview mirror, and my heart just sank! The vehicle was still there. What were they doing? Why were they doing it? I thought it was a coincidence the first time, and then it appeared they were always a few cars behind me everywhere I went.

After this happened again and again, I became panicky and called my friend Alesha. But I began to feel that I was bothering her far too much. She knew the pain and agony I suffered, and as my friend it was tremendously hard for her to hear these things. I did not want to affect her spiritual walk any further just because mine was shattered. She wanted me to calm down so that I wouldn't have another breakdown. I told her I would call her later.

Later I called her, right after I looked out of my patio window and saw a black Suburban this time outside of my home. She told me to call the police immediately. I didn't, because I was paralyzed with fear. I started turning off the lights and lying low in the condo. I was afraid, because I did not know what they were trying to do. I had felt so free and safe in that condo and I did not have a blind on my patio door window. I had a wooden fence out back, and I figured that nobody could see through there unless they were trying to.

From the time I had gotten kicked out of the church, I felt intimidated. Alesha would continuously tell me to call the police about the alleged stalking, but I didn't dare. I knew that if I dialed 911 and they wanted to harm me that I would be hurt before the police ever got there. That was my logic then, and I was thinking that since they had called me a security risk that maybe this was some standard procedure. I would be so scared that I stopped cooking in my kitchen because it was next to my patio door.

My son and I got quick-to-prepare foods like sandwiches, and we went to fast food restaurants just to avoid the kitchen. I even began to think whoever was following me might shoot me or that they wanted me dead. I started to let depression and fears rule my world. My son didn't realize what was going on at the time, but I knew that he was starting to feel uneasy. Our home was not our haven any more.

It got so bad that at night, when I drove into the complex, I would circle around it in my car. When I got out of my car, I went into the complex, walked through my front door, and had my son sit in the doorway until I checked the rooms in the dark. I did not want to turn the lights on. I kept my phone and knife close by, and I began to become a very light sleeper, when I got any sleep at all. I figured it was a good thing that I slept during the day, because that way I could be on alert all night. I could not understand why they would want to monitor me at night. During the day when I went out, it was typically to the market or for a job opportunity. Maybe they thought that I would go to the media in the middle of the night. I felt like they thought that I knew far too much information, and I began to understand why Pastor Michael was urging me to get out of town. I even understood that Jessica had me set up to get kicked out of the church so that I would leave ... perhaps she was trying to save me from her father. Well, this got to be too much for me, and I really knew that I had to go. It was like the Mafia. I was already dead in every way but physically, and

I was not trying to take any chances with my life. I had to live and to get better for my son.

I had to explain to my son once again that we were moving, but he did not want to move. He started to have dreams of doing commercials and working in the entertainment industry and we both were excited. I just knew that he had a great future with the entertainment industry, but those dreams for us were crushed by all of the victimization from this M A F I A ministry. I began receiving hang-up calls too, and I feared for my life! I figured either we move, or I am going to die there. I knew that these people wanted me to disappear. These people were twisted and sick. I believed this master manipulator was capable of anything.

Moving was hard. It was June of 2006. When we moved from Irvine, I had promised my son a better life and it had been hard for him to move from the Chicago area. I felt so alone and guilty; overwhelmingly guilty. I didn't understand any of the traumatic events, but my son was totally a soldier through it all. I know that God gave him the supernatural strength that he needed during that time. The way Pastor Benny fired me, and the way we were kicked out of the church after I had a breakdown from all that was happening with the ministry was devastating. And as if that was not enough, I didn't know that that abuse could be topped by intimidation. I left everything behind: my son's career, the housing program, my neighbors and my associates. I got away as fast as I could. I didn't have any more time to be harassed, or for people to play games with my life.

I knew that I didn't want to go back to Chicago, and I knew that I couldn't stay where I was. I felt a sense of urgency to get out of California. Oddly enough, I decided to go on to Texas. I shipped what we could to Texas and drove 23 hours straight. I didn't know much about Texas at all; in fact I had never been there except for riding through on an Amtrak train. I did a little more research and remembered some of what Pastor Michael had told me. I had a couple of cousins there, and one had told me that

I could stay with her until I found a place. That seemed to be the fastest and safest route.

I remember when we were driving through Arizona and my son was in his booster seat in the back, and suddenly he said, "Mom look! There go two rainbows, one dull one and one bright one." I looked up at the sky at the rainbows and was excited that he sounded cheerful. He said, "Mom, that means that God is telling us that the past is behind us and that our future is going to be brighter." I was floored. That was so phenomenal to hear from my 7-year-old son. I was speechless. I started to praise the Lord and thank Him in advance for what was in front of us.

11

REVICTIMIZATION

I felt safe once I left California. But when I arrived in Texas I was still a total mess. This was so much deeper than the other hurts that had happened during the course of my life. It had manipulated my mind, abused my soul, left me impoverished emotionally, financially, physically, but most of all, spiritually. My very being was intimidated, and it was all done with such arrogance. If you asked anyone that was involved in this situation, I am certain they would say that I was just a disgruntled employee.

My soul had been brutalized, and ironically Benny Hinn Ministries' theme for the year had been souls, souls, souls. They said that they wanted to win souls to Christ. In the midst I was trying to pick up the pieces of my life and didn't know what was where. Did they care about *my* soul? Once I got to Texas, I found myself at such a low point that I was suicidal, so I decided to reach out to pastors at other churches, as well as their wives and counselors. I reached out to televangelist ministries such as The Potters House with Pastor T.D. Jakes, Without Walls International with Paula White, Juanita Bynum ministries and local neighborhood churches. Anyone that I could talk to I did, because I was a lost sheep trying to find my way back to my true Master. I wanted to feel the fire of the Lord again; I was confused and lonely so I reached out … I didn't want to give up on church and pastors. I still believed that there was righteousness in ministry. I craved for righteousness in ministry, but a ministry that truly believed in living a Christ-like lifestyle and was sincere about it. Just one who had love and mercy. I believed that we are our brother's keeper, and that we are to be held accountable to each other and bear one another's burdens. I knew that there was no way I was going to give up on God. But I was tired of being tormented and not being able to sleep. I wanted to be free. I felt that I was in bondage.

I had become so isolated that I would talk to anyone who would listen. I reached out and little did I know that once again the snowball effect would throw the ultimate blow to my mind, body, and soul. I repeatedly talked on the phone and sat in the offices with pastors who were star struck and would have me go over the business of what happened at Benny Hinn's house in "confidence," just to turn around and tell me that I should "just lay it on the alter" and "pray about it."

They would pray for me. They would break curses off of my life. They would cast demons out of me. They would tell me to not touch God's anointed one and do His prophet no harm. They would tell me that they knew him and wouldn't believe such things. They would sweep it under the rug. They told me to keep quiet. They told me to never speak out because I would cause many of God's children to go astray because of who he was. They told me that Benny Hinn was an anointed man of God and that I had to go through that process to learn something. They told me to leave it alone and go on with my life. They told me that they had been through worse and that it was all a part of ministry. They told me that God's gifts are without repentance. They told me that I was out of order. They told me to not speak another word or I would bring a curse on my family.

They would tell me that I was being prepped for full-time ministry. They would tell me that God's anointing was on me, and I had Benny Hinn's mantel over me. They told me that I would minister to the nations. They would tell me that I was a prophetess. Then there were those that would want me to work in their ministries. They had me work in their ministries. They told me that I would do great things for the Lord. They told me that the Lord was teaching me how to be a servant. They prophesied over me. They held my hand. They told me that they would be there with me every step of the way …. They groomed me, they sexually assaulted me, and then a pastor in the Dallas area raped me. The cycle of revictimization in ministry started all over again. I reached out again to the church, and this time I was rocked to my already weakened core ….This is what pastors, their wives, and their counselors had to say to me: "Well what did you do to cause this?" "You must examine your heart, Cheryl." "Look at your shirt today, you are showing cleavage." A pastor's wife told me as I sat in her office one morning, in distress, shortly after the the rape, that one of the men working at her church asked, "What man is she looking for coming in here dressed like that?" Another pastor's wife said, "Oh girl, just put it on the altar, my mom was raped by her pastor."

Pastors continued to say, "You don't need counseling. Just give it to Jesus." "We all have a story." "It's all in God's plan." "Just get on with your life." "Just forgive and forget." "God will deal with him." "You don't have to say a thing." "Why didn't you go to the hospital right after?" "Why didn't you call the police right away?" "Why won't you give me his name?" "I hope that you weren't tempting the pastor." "Why are you protecting him?" "You act like you love him?" "Why would you talk to him after that?"

A pastor's wife from a mega church who was just plain ignorant told me of her affair with a married man at her place of employment, and how she got all sorts of diamonds out of him, and when she finally married the pastor she is with, she melted all of those diamonds to the huge rock she sports now … Here is what she had to say, which is so amusing to me now: "You wouldn't be attracted to a white pastor, would you? Well, we would get you some counseling if you were a member, but since you worked with Benny Hinn Ministries, can you help us host a Christian musical event that we are having at our church and help us bake Christmas cookies?"

There is so much that I could share, I even contacted New Birth Church with Pastor Eddie Long in Lithonia, GA after I was raped, they prayed for me and told me that the devil was very busy! I surely agreed with that. When I contacted the Dallas Baptist association about the matter, they immediately contacted the pastor that violated me, after I requested them not to, I found out when he called me and told me. Each of these organized religious institutions put me at greater risks covering for each other. This list could just go on and on and on. I must say that ignorance is bliss in a lot of traditional, religious, and cultic churches. One thing is for sure, they are all linked up and they got each other's back for sure. **M A F I A Ministry** *A Crying Shame*.

12

HEALING

I am still in the healing process. I have endured much hurt from my initiation into the M A F I A ministry. I have felt like these "ministries" killed me in so many areas of my life. I have worked from the storefronts to the forefronts of them. Hey, I know that there is no perfect "ministry," yet at this point in my life, I am no longer a part of any organized religious church. I feel it's a cheap way to exploit vulnerable Christians in America, and abroad, through organizations such as BHM. It seems that with a little good music, fun, and ear-tickling, predators begin to set up shop and prey on the vulnerable. What a happy place for the weak, lonely, abused, and unfortunate to give their all through works and money in hopes of being prosperous and getting into heaven! I am so happy that we now have a term for it: "spiritual" abuse. The name popped into my mind soon after coming out of BHM. I know that God gave me a revelation on that term.

I am learning to forgive beyond the surface. I realize that I suffer when I don't forgive, even if they never ask for forgiveness. I have forgiven the pastor that sexually violated me. He asked for forgiveness. I feel that if I never went through what I did at BHM that it would have never happened. I temporarily lost myself in the midst of it all.

I still have a personal relationship with God. I love Him with all of my heart, and the desire of my heart is to know Him more and do His will. I *did* try to become a member of several churches since Benny Hinn Ministries. But the minute that I recognize M A F I A ministry tactics, I am out of the building. I have zero tolerance for abuse in ministry or the churchy people who cover for them. I know that this exists and how real it is. It is not only devastating to the person being abused, but it reaches their friends and families as well. I have experienced many losses in relationships, socially and in my career, because of all of the issues associated with this matter.

I contacted Benny a few times before I had to write this book but he never responded. It has been almost five years since I left California. I do not consider BHM a ministry; I consider it to be a cult of which he is the leader, hiding under the guise of a minister or a healer. I do not believe anything he says. In fact Benny didn't belong to a church himself, when I was there. Benny has no accountability what so ever! I did not write this book to church bash! What they do has nothing to do with church or the healing power of Jesus. They are scammers, and nothing more.

I had so many people tell me to not write this book for fear of the backlash, but something opened up for me where the words just totally flowed, and I was able to get it out. I also realize that some of you love this man, and that is your choice. He is still one of God's children, and it is not too late for him to practice some of what he preaches, although that could even be confusing, since his teachings are so twisted.

If there are some fanatics reading this and you are upset, go to his website, and you can purchase a prosperity prayer shawl for $50 and/or a promise bracelet for $15, and pray for them. But please don't pray for me. Sometimes the more people decorate, the deeper they are hurt. This book has been very therapeutic for me. I have been in counseling the last year at my school and it has helped me tremendously. Texas Woman's University is the school that I was attending once I started to regain myself again; their counseling department has helped me to understand how to pick up the pieces again. On top of all my past abuse, I have had an eating disorder and financial hardships, and it has been an emotional roller coaster, but I am on the path to recovery.

My son is doing well. He is a very blessed young man, and I know that God has him in the palm of His hand and continues to give him supernatural strength each day. He does well in school, and everyone tells me that whatever I am doing with him I should keep doing it. I am very proud of him, and he keeps me on track. We both understand that because of the nature of this book, changes may be made in a lot of areas. I am preparing to deal with what's to come.

There is a fear that tries to creep in at times. But I will not let anything hinder my voice about these types of abuses anymore. I really am at a point where I don't care what a religious fanatic has to say about me. I am happy that a lot of wolves in sheep's' clothing are being exposed today, and I pray that the awareness will reach out like never before. A few of the ministries that I personally reached out to have been exposed; now I see why it was not meant for them to be a part of my life.

I truly believe that God has placed some people on this earth to expose and disclose certain things. You may not agree with everything that I have shared, but at this point to me, if it flowed out like that, then it is what it is. I will not be ashamed about it, nor will I retract it. This is about informing and healing. Definitely, when it all boils down, God is my ultimate source.

I know that God is a healer. I didn't pick up a Bible for years because of this master manipulating madness, but I was gullible. I pray that more Christians will become bold and stand and know when to recognize that whatever is oppressing you is not what God wants for your life. I have been wounded physically, emotionally, sexually, and spiritually from cultic ministries such as Benny Hinn's, and even if there is just one under the sound of my voice, my heart is for you to reach out by all means necessary.

When one door closes, knock on another and another, until your voice is heard or maybe you should write a book. I had to look on internet sites and find books to read pertaining to the issues that I was trying to cope with. If you encounter a person that is hurting in this manner, whether you are "clergy" or not, please direct them to the proper help immediately. Please do not give them your personal opinion of the situation if they are in crisis, as it can cause more damage than good. And to victims: don't be intimidated by these predators. I know that there is a very special place in Hell for "pastors" like this who do not make it right.

I want anyone who is involved in any abusive situation to reach out, educate yourself, and know that if you have been abused as a child sexually, physically, emotionally, or otherwise, that you are more prone to this type of abuse as an adult. When you reach out to a "ministry" or they reach out to you, for anything, you must beware of those who use the guise of religion to further distribute abuse. Be on the lookout for M A F I A Ministry A Crying Shame.

Cheryl Brown

June 16, 2009

Pastor Benny Hinn

Dana Pointe, CA _ _°

Dear Benny Hinn:

After much prayer and thought I, Cheryl Brown feel a moral and spiritual responsibility to address the matter at hand. First, I would like to state that after being referred to work for you and your family, by your daughter, Jessica Hinn-Koulianos, I felt honored. Being under her and Pastor Michael Koulianos direction, I believed that I was doing God's will being a servant to one of His chosen vessels. I am confident that you have not forgotten my son,   and I when I worked for you as your personal housekeeper from 2005 through 2006. We developed a personal relationship with you and your family. I am coming forward about the way I was treated during and after my employment at your home (parsonage). This is still very difficult for me and I am going to list a few details which are still a constant trauma that effects me emotionally, physically, mentally but most of all spiritually. In January of 2006, on my off day, I returned to the parsonage with the intent to discuss with you the fact that you had not paid me my earnings that were owed to me in over 4 weeks.

"Deuteronomy 24:15
15"You shall give him his wages on his day before the sun sets, for he is poor and sets his heart on it; so that he will not cry against you to the LORD and it become sin in you.

When I tried to explain to you how difficult it had been for me to not get paid on time, you became irate and disrespectful. I had endured verbal attacks from your wife, I was promised money and other employment opportunities with Pastor Ralph Wilkerson, and I was disappointed with a host of other practices and actions that are too painful for me to relive at this moment. But when you proceeded to scold me and express your pure contempt towards me because I simply needed to be paid for my earnings. I was in shock. After you threw me out of your home and slammed the door behind me so hard that I thought the door would break, I stood on the stairs of your beautiful home in disbelief and I cried. I walked to my car and drove away emotionally distraught because you treated me as if I was garbage.

*Micah 6:8
He has showed you, O man, what is good. And what does the LORD require of you? To act justly and to love mercy and to walk humbly with your God.

Shortly after the incident at your home, I was intimidated later by your security team who followed me around,   and physically removed me and my son from the church. Your security team told me that "I and my son were no longer welcome at the World Healing Center Church and that I was considered a security risk and that they were simply doing what they were asked to do." My son was completely traumatized by this. How was I supposed to explain to my son who was 7 years old at the time that we were just kicked out of his church? For no reason, the intimidation lasted   months and my son and I were so scared, emotionally distraught and overwhelmed that I suffered several breakdowns. The intimidation   and other staff telling me

"It's all about Benny Hinn and his family because he is untouchable and to never go against the ministry or that I will be cursed." I just could not take it anymore and since I was too scared to call the police, I packed up me and my son's belongings and relocated to Texas. I would like to emphasize that it has taken me 3 plus years to come forward. Benny Hinn, as a result of the   that had occurred in your home, the termination, the humiliation and intimidation I endured while still living in the Orange County area you caused my son and I   caused me to seek therapy and counseling. Again it has taken over 3 years for me to finally have the strength and courage to tell you how much pain and suffering you have caused us. I am now set free from the spirit of fear and the spirit of control that had me bound all this time. I will continue to seek help for my son and I until we are whole once again. I come to you boldly but also in love and in peace. I feel that monetary compensation is appropriate for the pain and suffering that has occurred as a result of your actions. I would like to request and schedule a time to discuss this matter in more detail.

*Matthew 18:15-17

15"If your brother sins against you, go and show him his fault, just between the two of you. If he listens to you, you have won your brother over. 16 But if he will not listen, take one or two others along, so that 'every matter may be established by the testimony of two or three witnesses. 17 If he refuses to listen to them, tell it to the church; and if he refuses to listen even to the church, treat him as you would a pagan or a tax collector.

I would like to resolve this matter amicably and expeditiously. My expectation is to agree on a settlement amount to satisfy damages. Please contact me within 14 days from the date of this letter. If I do not hear from you within 14 days, I will have to pursue other measures to resolve this matter. I would like to move on with my life and put this behind us. I look forward to hearing from you.

*Matthew 18:6

6 But if anyone causes one of these little ones who believe in me to sin, it would be better for him to have a large millstone hung around his neck and to be drowned in the depths of the sea.

Sincerely yours,

Cheryl Brown

My letter to pastor benny

Thank you Jesus

When I woke to the sun shining
All I could do was smile
Thank the Lord for another day
And knelt to pray for a little while
During the course of my day
My hands I had to raise
Crying tears of joy
To the Lord I had to praise
I had to tell him thank you
For helping me go through
All the pain and sorrow
Without you
I wouldn't know what to do
Thank you Jesus
For being there through the storms
Thank you Jesus
For keeping me safe in your arms
Thank you Jesus
For being my father, now I'm not fatherless
Thank you Jesus
For bringing out my best
Thank you Jesus
It's good to know you'll always be here
Thank you Jesus
Thank you

- Cheryl Brown

SPECIAL THANKS TO

MY FRIEND ALESHA,
ARGLENDA FRIDAY,
CAITLIN MCLELLAN AND
DENISE MILLER

ACKNOWLEDGEMENTS

I THANK GOD FOR HIS UNCONDITIONAL LOVE, CONSTANT PROVISION AND PROTECTION.

I WOULD LIKE TO THANK MY MOTHER FOR BIRTHING ME INTO THE WORLD.

I WANT TO THANK MY SON FOR BEING MY NUMBER ONE FAN AND LAUGHING AT ALL OF MY JOKES ☺ I LOVE YOU WITH ALL OF MY HEART AND I AM VERY PROUD OF YOU! ALWAYS REMEMBER THAT YOU CAN DO ALL THINGS THROUGH CHRIST WHICH STRENGTHENS YOU!

References

FORGIVING THE UNFORGIVABLE
BY DAVID STOOP, PHD

*HEALING THE HURTING/GIVING HOPE AND
HELP TO ABUSED WOMEN* BY CATHERINE
CLARK KROEGER & JAMES R. BECK

NATIONALEATINGDISORDERS.ORG (NEDA)

*NO MORE HURTING/LIFE BEYOND
SEXUAL ABUSE* BY GWEN PURDIE

PUREPROVENDER.BLOGSPOT.COM

*REACHING THE HURTING/A BIBLICAL GUIDE FOR
HELPING ABUSE VICTIMS BY* SAMANTHA NELSON

*SEXUAL MISCONDUCT IN COUNSELING
AND MINISTRY* BY PETER MOSGOFIAN
AND GEORGE OHLSCHLAGER

SPIRITUALABUSE.COM

SPIRITUALABUSE.ORG

*SUICIDEPREVENTIONLIFELINE.ORG
OR PHONE* 1-800-273-8255(TALK)

1-800-784-2433 (SUICIDE)
1-800-799-4889 (4TTY) (HEARINGIMPAIRED)

THE UNCAGEDED PROJECT/SOUL STRATEGIES TO RISE ABOVE A WOUNDED CHILDHOOD BY SALLIE CULBRETH

WWW.CHURCHABUSE.COM

WWW.THEHOPEOFSURVIVORS.COM

211 RESOURCES FOR TRAINING, EMPLOYMENT, AN AGING PARENT, HOUSING OPTIONS, ADDICTION PREVENTION, SUPPORT GROUPS, FOOD PANTRIES AND MORE

NOTES